MAKE MINE

A DOUBLE

THE LOCKDOWN LEGENDS
ST JOHNSTONE FC: 2020/21

ED HODGE

First published in 2021 by

ARENA SPORT
An imprint of Birlinn Limited
West Newington House
10 Newington Road
Edinburgh
EH9 1QS

www.arenasportbooks.co.uk

Text copyright © Ed Hodge, 2021

ISBN: 9781913759025
eBook ISBN: 9781788854757

British Library Cataloguing-in-Publication Data
A catalogue record for this book is available on request from the British Library.

Designed and typeset by Polaris Publishing, Edinburgh

Printed and bound in Great Britain by Clays Ltd, Elcograf S.p.A.

CONTENTS

ACKNOWLEDGEMENTS

In an unthinkable period of our lives, our club did the unthinkable. The most incredible cup double, perhaps in the entire history of Scottish football. Astounding, miraculous, unbelievable – it is difficult to find one adjective. It was an achievement for the ages. After witnessing relegation and continual struggles to escape from the First Division, I get goosebumps thinking about season 2020-21 – the greatest season in the club's history.

To surpass the achievement of Scottish Cup glory in 2014 has been remarkable for everyone of a St Johnstone affiliation. After all, as supporters we all craved that day on 17 May, *Our Day in May*. Finally, after 130 years of long waiting, we had our hands on a major national trophy. Generations of Saints fans never saw such a scene. Having supported Saints since 1989 when McDiarmid Park opened its doors, and witnessed many an up and down, I admit to shedding a tear or two amid the joyous scenes.

The fact I did so alongside my late father, Kenneth, who passed away in 2017, will always mean that day holds added poignancy. For almost 30 years, virtually every time we took in a Saints game we did so together. A father and son bond, like so many football fans enjoy.

In dad's final months in late 2016, I managed to arrange for him to meet Tommy Wright and Callum Davidson for a coffee and a football chat after team training one day at the University of Stirling. It was emotional, yet a day to raise his spirits. Dad was hugely proud of both men for what they had achieved at Saints. His beaming smile at Celtic Park on 17 May 2014 was testament to that.

Over the last year, I've thought about dad and the other Saints no longer with us – perhaps victims of the Covid-19 pandemic – who have missed out on witnessing Callum and the team writing their names into Perth folklore. A couple double, pure fantasy football.

Without wanting to sound negative, there is every likelihood it will never happen again, such is the scale of the achievement of a small, provincial, family-run club winning the two major domestic cup trophies on offer in Scottish football. Winning any silverware in Scotland – traditionally outside of Celtic, Rangers, Hearts, Hibernian and Aberdeen – is an incredibly difficult goal to achieve. Elsewhere, finances are stronger, fan bases bigger, expectation higher.

As much as this book is about chronicling a simply remarkable season for all of us – mainly witnessed in front of laptops, mobile phones and TVs – it is for those Saints no longer here who missed out on seeing a wee team from Perth triumph twice at Hampden inside three months. The fans' section at the back of this book highlights what the season meant to so many, including contributions from Stuart Cosgrove, Eilidh Barbour, Colin McCredie, Jo Wilson and Nick Dasovic.

For everyone, it's been a hugely challenging period. The devastating loss of loved ones, near and far. Lockdowns. Masks. Home schooling. Home working. Our lives turned upside down. Prayers. Claps. Our health workers, our true champions.

St Johnstone helped to raise a smile, and more, in the Covid-19 world. It was life behind a screen, two hours out of mundane days broken up to cheer on the Saints. From worry and head scratching up to Christmas 2020, to pure joy for the final five months of the season. Such has been the bonus of regular live games, including through SaintsTV, I arguably watched more of Saints in the last season than ever before – just not in person. Live football sustained so many of us in the dark times.

I'm sure similar scenes were repeated by the majority of die-hard Saints near and far. Tuning in to PeterheadTV on a dreary November day for a key Betfred League Cup win; superstitiously sitting in the same positions in the living room for the cup semi-finals and finals (my wife, Iona, and my children, Andrew and Kirsty, questioning my sanity!); or screaming from the lungs 'Zander has scored!' on a late Sunday evening before the final episode of *Line of Duty* (well, nearly Zander). There were tense, blood pressure through the roof days, with one of the few benefits of lockdown being that we were able to watch many of the games as a family, sharing hopes, sharing dreams, sharing the silverware scenes.

My son, Andrew, has a great passion for Arsenal but now appears hooked on the Saints too – having witnessed the club lift three major trophies before even hitting his teenage years!

During it all there were WhatsApp groups to maintain the Saints following, regular messages fired off to my old Crieff High School friend, Stuart Woods, now in Kent, or my brother-in-law, Neil Robertson, down in Surrey. Messages of support were also sent to Callum, Steven MacLean and Liam Craig. I count myself fortunate to have stayed in contact with such talented, respected individuals going back several years.

After the final whistle blew against Hibs in the Scottish Cup Final, I soon felt the desire to take on another project like

Our Day in May. I was actually keen to write another book in lockdown but couldn't settle on an idea, so this has been the ultimate labour of love – going behind the scenes and allowing each player and the management to share stories from the most incredible year of their footballing lives. I thank Hugh Andrew, the Managing Director at Birlinn Ltd, for quickly buying into the concept and helping turn this book around over a few short months – just as we did with *Our Day in May*. My thanks also to Peter Burns at Polaris Publishing, who assists Hugh on projects, and has also been subject to various 'are you following this Saints story!?' messages.

My sincere gratitude also to Steve Brown, Chairman, and Roddy Grant at Saints for supporting my draft idea back in June, with Steve no doubt delighted to no longer be pestered by my regular calls. A big thanks to Callum and 'Macca' for their generous time for interviews and access to all the players, past and present. I'm due Callum a game of golf in return! Thanks too to Sam Porter at the club for his help and Graeme Hart for his wonderful images.

Gordon Bannerman rode to the rescue to help me track down players who have since moved on, while Janette Dewar was a great help with her expert proof reading. Liz Dexter was also a wonderful assistance in transcribing many an interview. A word too for another journalist, Robert Thomson, on his 'Lockdown Legends' idea.

Lastly, a big thanks to my mum, Nicola, sister, Geraldine, and to Iona and the kids for always being supportive and driving me on. Pulling together 68,000 words in two months (mainly at night!) was a challenge, but job done!

Since 2009, when Derek McInnes brought Saints back to Scotland's top division on that sunny afternoon with a win over Morton, the level of achievement at the club has been extraordinary. Callum, though, has topped the lot. Enjoy reading this truly astonishing football tale. A story for any underdog to aspire to. A story that may never be written again.

Ed Hodge
August 2021

STEVE BROWN, CHAIRMAN

It's well-known my dad, Geoff, saved the club 35 years ago. He was just making sure there was a club in Perth, one for the community to continue to support. What you have seen, certainly over the last 10 years or so, nobody could ever have imagined. It took us 130 years to win one cup in 2014 and then we win two in the one season, two in a matter of months! It's been hard to register, to be honest. Doing it in the middle of a global pandemic certainly gave us all something to smile about, during hugely difficult times for us all. On top of that, we did so well to finish strongly, claim fifth in the league and secure the club's return to Europe. Again, that didn't really sink in until we were travelling to Turkey to take on a side like Galatasaray. What an experience that was.

It really has been a truly remarkable period for St Johnstone. The amount of time, effort and sacrifices we all put in is considerable, with a lot of disappointments along the way, so to get some rewards for it, from 35 years, it's been a special time. Will it ever sink in? I'm not sure it ever will. It's difficult for me to describe it without getting too emotional, to be honest.

We're up against it every year in Scotland, as the Old Firm are miles ahead of everyone else. Clubs like Aberdeen, Hearts and

Hibernian also have far bigger budgets than us. For us to even get to a cup final, I know that sounds a little negative, takes a huge effort from Callum and all the players. To therefore get to two cup finals, hold our nerve and win both matches, well, it may never be done again by a club the size of ours – it's as simple as that. It's been a remarkable achievement and I'm proud of everyone involved – Callum, the players, the club staff and, of course, the fans. Savour this time, celebrate it and never forget it.

Of course, I was especially delighted for Callum to do the double. It's incredible now looking back to that period at the start of the season as we struggled for wins. Some people might have just looked at the results, which were mixed, but for me, we were consistent. We performed well in almost every game. We just didn't get the results as often as we deserved. We went through a run when we weren't scoring and there were one or two unfortunate refereeing decisions that didn't go our way.

For Callum, following Tommy (Wright) was inevitably a big challenge straight away. But Callum's taken it in his stride. No manager we've employed has had the challenges he's been faced with in terms of Covid-19. It's not just keeping the players fit and playing. Things can happen out with our bubble that you have no control over. But he's strong and he's come through it. If I didn't think he was any good I wouldn't have appointed him! We had some good chats when he was at Millwall and I'm so pleased he decided to return north, given his success under Tommy as an assistant here. We knew his calibre and all the traits that we thought would stand him in good stead have done just that – his personality, playing career, his coaching experience and working with Scotland. His first year in the job and he wins two cup finals – he has a huge task now to top it!

Obviously, the sad part of the 2020-21 season was not having you, our fans, to witness both cup successes. It was a massive disappointment fans couldn't be there, but we knew why they couldn't be. It wasn't safe to do so, it's as simple as that. For all you at home watching the finals on a screen, I'm sure it didn't take away from the excitement leading up to the Hampden contests and the emotions we all go through during the games themselves.

It goes without saying that, in terms of the experience of watching cup finals at Hampden, it was nothing like it would have been with you there. But the emotions don't change, it was still fantastic. It was nice to hug my dad after the Hibs win and just take it all in. It was a hugely emotional time. It's what dreams are made of. That's why I'm in the game, why the manager and players are – and it is what you, as supporters, want for the team. It's the ambition for everybody.

Callum was good enough to remind me before the Livingston final that we didn't have a very good record at Hampden, which I was trying to forget. Mind you, the same applied to our record of never having won the Scottish Cup – just because we hadn't done it in the past didn't mean we couldn't win it in 2014 and it was the same against Livi, and then Hibs.

With a combination of good managers, good players, good luck and a bit of good judgment it's been an extraordinary tenure for me since taking over as Chairman in 2011. As much as there have been times when I've had my challenges, I couldn't have asked for any more. I really couldn't.

It's great looking back at things, even the signing of Shaun Rooney. Roddy Grant and I went to watch a Dundee-Inverness match with an eye on an Inverness player, who didn't have his best game it's fair to say. But obviously we saw this big, athletic wing-back marauding up and down the line. He couldn't be stopped and we thought 'wow, here is a player'. We came back and reported to Tommy, got him on a pre-contract and the rest is history!

Fast forward and I celebrated for three days after the Scottish Cup win! I had a combination of feelings. Firstly, elation, that sense of achievement at the end of the season. Then there was the Covid situation, which we had for the whole season. Unless you were directly involved, it is hard to relate to how challenging it was. Family-wise, it was a big moment too. My dad tried for years to get the holy grail, to win a cup. For him to see a double delivered, it was just amazing. It stands to reason you're going to be a wee bit tearful.

I went on to about 5.40am at the stadium! My Fitbit told me I then went to sleep! I woke up about 8.30am and called my wife for a lift home! I had a christening at 12 o'clock, then it was off to the Cherrybank Inn as the manager, players and directors were there. That was a late night! The next day we went to Gleneagles for 'lunch' and back to Perth! Great times.

It's also been great to see the pride in Perth for this team. It's the same as I remember from the Scottish Cup Final in 2014, everybody's talking about the club again, even people who aren't into football. It's the same buzz. It puts Perth on the map again. We're in the media, on the television and being talked about. The players get a lift from it and a sense of achievement. Our current season ticket holders have given the team great backing, new holders have joined and, of course, we would love to see even more of you to support this club!

Aberdeen were the last non-Old Firm club to do the domestic double over 30 years ago. Between getting into Europe, top-six finishes and now winning two cups in one year, it is beyond what my dad was considering when he took the club on all those years ago.

As I've said, I don't think our double will be matched, not when you look at the strength of the Old Firm and other bigger teams. It's really a time to savour and one we will remember for the rest of our lives. Raise a glass to the Perth Saints and enjoy this story of our success. The words are there for evermore.

ONE

PERTH RETURN

'There's a freshness and enthusiasm about Callum.
Everyone speaks highly of him'
Gordon Strachan

All good things have to come to an end (or so we thought).
2 May 2020: Newsflash . . .
    'Tommy Wright has quit as St Johnstone manager after seven years
in charge' (BBC online)

Tommy Wright
I felt that when you're at a club for such a length of time sometimes there just comes a point when you need a break. It was something being considered for a while.

We made the decision that we would see, in the next couple of years, if we could bring the age of the squad down and then it might be time for me to move on. Fortunately, we've done that. I'm extremely proud of the situation I leave the club in. There are lots and lots of memories. Even things that people don't think about, like the loads of young players I gave their debut to. Over the last couple of days I've had time to reflect and

I've remembered people like Zander (Clark), Jason (Kerr), Liam (Gordon) and Ali (McCann).

Thinking back, I had a sense of foreboding at the date anyhow. Saturday 2 May 2020 had been pencilled in for one of those Covid-19 lockdown projects that parents of young children quickly began to dread – building a new trampoline. With little progress made on the instruction manual inside the first hour – head scratching and hand bruising my main accomplishment before my wife and kids ably excelled – the regular beeping on my mobile phone was at least a pleasant distraction from the morning's DIY. Then it hit me – Tommy was gone. It was time up for St Johnstone's (then) greatest ever gaffer. What a day this was turning out to be.

Rarely in football does a manager depart to an outpouring of affection, but the afternoon highlighted just that towards the 58-year-old. He had delivered the club's first major trophy in 130 years, regular top-six finishes and European jaunts (including the scalp of Rosenborg) and Twitter even called for the renaming of McDiarmid Park's East Stand in Tommy's honour. Saints securing a third successive fourth-place finish under Wright in the Scottish Premiership in 2016-17 says it all about the job the affable Northern Irishman did.

Liam Craig, Midfielder and Vice-Captain, 34

I couldn't believe it. I'd spoken to the manager a lot in those few months when the season had finished in March, and then I had a missed call, at quarter to nine on a Saturday. I was on a morning run and I thought 'I'll just phone him when I get in.' That was him phoning me to tell me it was getting announced at 11 o'clock. I felt good about the fact that he wanted to do that (give me advanced notice) – it showed how much he held me in high regard as well – but it was a massive shock.

Amid the surprise timing, Wright's departure maintained a familiar trend for St Johnstone – managers moving on with the club's blessing following sterling work. Owen Coyle. Derek McInnes. Steve Lomas. Tommy Wright. The last time Saints actually sacked a manager was way back in April 2005, then bringing to an end the brief and disappointing tenure of club legend John Connolly. A conveyor belt of five successful managers have followed across the ensuing 16 years, a statistic almost unheard of in the modern game. Hearts, for example, have employed 15 managers within the same timeframe.

The level of Saints' success has obviously aided managerial longevity. Since returning to the top flight in 2009 thanks to First Division title glory under McInnes, the club has secured eight top-six finishes and sealed six European qualifications. It's simply unparalleled for St Johnstone.

Alex Cleland, First-Team Coach, 50

Tommy came to me and said 'Alex, I'm going to be leaving the club.' I was shocked. He was like 'no, I've made up my mind. I have my reasons. I've been here a long time.' He just felt it was the right time. The Chairman (Steve Brown) asked me to take over, said I had been here a long time too (since 2009), knew what he expected from me and that he trusted me. I knew the club, the players and had worked with Tommy, as well as being part of the first-team with Steve (Lomas) and Derek (McInnes). I said I was willing to do it (be caretaker manager), had done it before at other clubs and felt I had the respect of the players. But I knew in my own mind the job wasn't for me. It's a great job and Tommy had said to me to go for it, but I didn't see myself as a manager. I like what I'm doing, working with younger players and coming in and out of the first-team when needed. I said, 'I think I've found my niche with the Under-18s and helping the manager when needed.' I straight away said to the Chairman I didn't want to be considered for the job. I said I wanted to stay at the club, be part of it, but would do it until we found the manager. The Chairman was happy with that. I enjoy what I'm doing, have experienced it for many years and didn't want the manager role full-time.

While there were platitudes for Wright, the football world never stops spinning. Within hours of his exit, the club's record £1.75m transfer to Blackburn Rovers in 1998 and the man who was assistant to Wright for the club's 2014 Scottish Cup triumph, was quickly installed as the favourite to make the journey back to Perth. By 18 June, it was rubber-stamped – it was time for Callum Davidson to return home. On a three-year deal, it was too good an opportunity for the former Scotland international defender to turn down. The Dunblane lad was heading back north.

Davidson, 45, had learnt his trade for five years as assistant to Wright (and notably with Gordon Strachan in the Scotland set up) before coaching spells with Stoke City, Dunfermline Athletic and latterly at Championship play-off-chasing Millwall, assisting his ex-Leicester team-mate Gary Rowett. 'He goes with our blessings and I think he'll do a really, really good job,' said Rowett of his friend. Davidson felt he had waited three to four years to be his own man, to call the shots, to make his own decisions. Now was his chance, back on familiar McDiarmid Park turf.

Callum Davidson, Manager
It was a difficult decision. We had started to put Millwall on an upward curve, after going in with Gary. The club was a breath of fresh air. I had some harder times at Stoke so I think going in there reinvigorated my real joy for coaching and football. It was a fantastic group of players and we felt we were onto something good. I had a great relationship with Gary and Joe (Carnall). I was living in a flat in London, commuting up and down the road, the flight and travel was easy. The family came down and

everyone knows London is a great place to visit. It was actually easier travel compared to Stoke. The flight was 45 minutes and I did work at the airports. It was pre-Covid and it actually took me about three hours from door to door sometimes.

When Tommy left it was a bit of a surprise to everybody because he had been there for so long and he seemed quite settled there. Then I obviously got the phone call from the Chairman. I'm not sure whether it was an interview, or just a chat like we used to do when I was an assistant, chatting about football and certain things. By the end of it, he just said, 'right then, so when are you coming up?' I kind of went 'is that you offering me the job?' It was a follow-up conversation as I had already spoken to Gary about the possibility of going. Gary was brilliant, to be fair. He was the one that sort of made my mind up. He didn't want me to go, as obviously we are good friends, but he knew management was a thing I wanted to do. He would have liked me there for four or five years more, but he just said it was an opportunity I couldn't turn down. He made a really good point, he said, 'you're going to be one of the 12 managers in the top league in Scotland'. When he put it that way, he made it sound like it was an easy decision, but of course it wasn't an easy decision. I really enjoyed Millwall, really enjoyed the job I was in.

By the end of the phone call with the Chairman and me asking if he was offering me the job, he said, 'of course, I am'. After he said that it was pretty simple to get things sorted. From that point on, it was a big thanks to Millwall, but I had a new chapter to look forward to. Covid-19 was obviously hitting us at that point, and I knew there were challenges ahead, but I was excited to get started.

Paul Mathers, Goalkeeping Coach, 51

It was in 2015 when Tommy brought me to the club (from a Rangers academy role) after Steve Banks left. If you look at what

Tommy did in his last, probably, two years at the club, he started to change the squad. We could see the fruits of that coming. Jamie McCart came in January 2020, (Shaun) Rooney was then due to come in the summer (on a pre-contract).

Liam Gordon, Defender, 25
It would have been such a daunting job for anyone to come after Tommy's success – arguably one of the club's greatest ever managers – in delivering the first major trophy for the club. I just think Callum's the only manager that could have come in, the only manager that could come in and could do better than that. We had come across him before when he was assistant, we knew exactly what he was going to bring to the club – like intensity to training just goes up that level, just the person he is around the place, so enthusiastic all the time. I felt like it was just time for a change.

Jason Kerr, Defender and Captain, 24
A thing people don't realise, as well, is that obviously in 2014 the club won the cup and Tommy was the manager, he would take the credit for it. But Callum was assistant manager and the training sessions he put on . . .

Liam Gordon
. . . were instrumental.

Jason Kerr
Yeah, the enthusiasm Callum put into training for the boys, I think that would have had a huge effect on them winning the Scottish Cup in 2014, because he was massive around the club when he was there. I loved it when he was there, and obviously, I was a bit disappointed when he left.

Liam Gordon

To the guys, he's just never half-job: everything's full or nothing with him. And it's whatever he does in life, I think that's what happens, that's the effect he has, and that's why he gets so much success.

Callum Davidson

I was probably hoping the call was going to come – at some stage. I spent five years with Tommy, five fantastic years at St Johnstone, but I wanted to sort of experience other things. If I was going to be a manager, it was a bit of a risk to leave. I kind of thought if I had stayed and Tommy had left then I might then have got the job straight away.

For me, it was for development and I think it's probably the best decision I made on my football side (leaving Saints in 2018 to become first-team coach at Stoke). For me, learning is a big one. I think Dunfermline (in 2019) would have probably surprised everybody when I went there. But I had just left Stoke and I wanted to enjoy coaching, and Stevie (Crawford) asked me to come and help him. I thought it was a great opportunity. I'm not one of these guys that thinks I'm bigger than anyone else, I just love coaching and love trying to get players to improve. With Gordon (Strachan), it was a brilliant experience. People ask me about the most special goal you have witnessed and one is probably from that time (Leigh Griffiths for Scotland against England in 2017 at Hampden). I still, to this day, remember Mark McGhee turning round to me going, 'He's going to score, he's going to score, he's going to score.' I think it was probably the second free-kick. I'm going, 'Mark, be quiet, he's not going to score, it's about 30 yards out'! And Leigh just stuck it in the net. The two of us just started laughing. The place went wild. That experience with Gordon, dealing with international players, now I have an idea of international football and what sort of ideas I would have to go forward there.

David Wotherspoon, Midfielder, 31

It was such an easy transition. Callum knows the club inside-out and it didn't take him long to slot in. It's his first managerial role and it was a big thing for him, but it just felt like he had always been there. We had him, obviously, as an assistant manager before, so we knew what he was about. It was very exciting as we always enjoyed his level of work and his training. He's a great guy as well, so it was certainly something I was looking forward to.

Jamie McCart, Defender, 24

It came as a bit of a surprise when Tommy left. I think it shocked everyone. When the new gaffer came in – obviously he had been here before with a few of the boys – but for most of us it was like a clean slate. So, I was actually really excited because I had spoken to Mikey (O'Halloran), Zander (Clark), who had worked with him as an assistant, and they said, 'you're going to love him, you're going to love how he plays'. I was quite looking forward to it.

Davidson quickly built his backroom team. With Mathers in place, Cleland became first-team coach with fans' favourite Steven MacLean – a 2014 cup final goal hero – a popular choice as a new first-team coach too, after his release from Hearts. MacLean, who scored 53 goals in 198 appearances for Saints, hung up his boots to focus on his new challenge.

Steven MacLean, First-Team Coach, 39

I was obviously excited when Callum phoned me. I was probably going to go to Raith Rovers and play for another year. But I'm getting on in years, so it was quite an easy decision to give up playing and take that next step as I always wanted to do it. Obviously coming back to St Johnstone, a club I know well, everything sort of fitted into place for me.

Alex Cleland

You never know with a new manager coming in what his thoughts are going to be. Callum has worked with a lot of good coaches so could have brought anyone in. I have been at Saints a long time and Alan Maybury was there as well, at the time. I was fortunate maybe because I had worked with Callum before, he knew what I could do with the Under-18s and knew that I could do both roles. I was delighted that he wanted to keep me and to work with him again. I knew how good a coach he was when he was assistant manager. I had a lot of good times with him before he left to go down south.

Callum was also keen to bring somebody in, but not make big changes. So 'Macca' (MacLean) came in and he saw us both as first-team coaches, as well as us both helping the Under-18s. It seemed a good mix. Macca had fresh new ideas, which has been great having just finished playing, Callum, with the experience he has from down south, integrated with the experience I've had with the Under-18s and all the managers I've worked with at St Johnstone. I think that was part of Callum's thinking, knowing that I knew the club and many of the players. I think I've found my role and I'm happy with it.

Callum Davidson

I worked with Macca and knew him very well. It's a strength I probably don't quite have in front of goal. I look at different aspects. Alex has got a brilliant nature about him. He has got a fantastic way of working, especially with the younger players. Macca was probably similar to myself when Tommy took over and I thought he had a lot to give the club. He has obviously played a big part in club history, as we know. But it wasn't a sentimental decision, it was a decision for the team and the best for St Johnstone.

MacLean's influence as a former penalty-box striker, a player who once formed a prolific partnership with Stevie May, could not be overestimated – especially as the season wore on.

Stevie May, Forward, 28

It's obviously different with Macca, completely different, in terms of he's not on the pitch going mental at everyone and being the Macca that we know! He kind of does it from the sidelines now. I think the more people you're familiar with and you get on with, it can only be beneficial, and St Johnstone has been a club that has been good with that throughout the whole time since I was a young boy here. Through the years, they have always kept people who have done well, and I think it speaks volumes if you all know the club inside out, the values, what it takes to play here and work hard for everyone. Macca's working as hard as ever, just in a different role now.

Chris Kane, Forward, 27

Obviously, as a striker, you want to score as many goals as you can, but when the manager came in he said he wanted us to defend from the front and for the strikers to do a lot of the hard work. He said, 'If you do that and perform well, then you'll keep yourself in the team.' He wants me to run, press, hold the ball up and that's what I feel like I've been doing. Obviously, he rewarded me by keeping me in the team so long. The goals are obviously bonuses, but I need to do that work right first.

Paul Mathers

Sometimes the job was consuming Tommy, as such, and he took it all on his shoulders. He always came back with a plan and the energy to just go again. We had a great run again before Covid hit, three defeats in 18 games, and he had put the base of a new team in place. Then Callum came in and with just that wee change, the direction on the pitch, it started to come together.

Steven MacLean

The Chairman has always wanted that sort of seamless transition with managers. That's what it was, although Callum is different. He has changed things, as we do play differently from Tommy's teams and sides in the past. That's testament to Callum, how good a coach he is and how good a manager he is. But it was important that he knew what the club is all about, as it always helps.

TWO

SLOW START

'Football without fans is nothing'
Jock Stein

Late July 2020. A global pandemic continued to grip our everyday lives. As countries edged in and out of 'lockdowns' or sought other means to try and tackle the ravages of Covid-19, football seemed less relevant amid the fight for life and death. Yet, for so many, it did matter. It offered a boost to mental health, giving fans a focus within the confines of their own four walls; something to look forward to within the daily grind. Of course, Scottish football's resumption allowed elite footballers to continue their careers amid the most challenging of circumstances.

Back in mid-May, amid heated domestic discussions, Celtic were crowned 2019-20 champions after a decision to end the season early due to the pandemic. While relegated Hearts threatened legal action, four points behind second-bottom Hamilton with both having eight games left, St Johnstone edged into the top six ahead of Hibs by points per game up to the last match played on 13 March.

A new season at least lay in wait for players in the Covid world, albeit with the continued absence of fans. After Rangers lost 3-1 to

Bayer Leverkusen on the evening of 12 March (in front of 47,494 supporters), the shutters soon went up across the country. Only fleeting flickers of light for supporters followed. A small handful of test events took place during the new campaign, but the maximum number of 500 was spread sparsely across vast oceans of empty plastic seats. It was to be life in front of a screen for fans, with clubs at least proactive in activating or improving their own club TV outputs to connect with their at-home supporters – Saints TV among them.

Liam Craig

Nothing beats that roar, that 10 seconds after you score, with such a big crowd behind you. I've been lucky: some of the goals I've scored, we've had a big following that day or a decent support at home, so to have no fans there was a massive loss.

Callum Davidson

Throughout the whole season, Covid-19 is probably the hardest thing I've had to deal with. When it came to how we trained there were a lot of things we couldn't implement. But I knew the spirit in the dressing room – or the six dressing rooms we were in all season. On training days, we were basically in six dressing rooms, to keep the players socially distanced. I knew it was difficult, but that was the hardest thing. We had games getting called off, we had the worry of testing, people isolating. It was a real, real difficult thing. I keep saying to Jim Fleeting (ex-Director of Coaching at the SFA) 'why didn't you teach me this in the Pro Licence?!' I keep texting him.

We were fortunate to still be doing our jobs. But all the players have had to live through very difficult times, what with social distancing and trying to avoid Covid outbreaks. They've had to live their lives really, really strictly and really watch what they're doing. I know we all have been, but players get scrutinised. If they catch Covid and do anything wrong then it's always in the papers. It's been really tough, but all credit to my boys for that. I think they were brilliant throughout the whole season.

David Wotherspoon
It was a strange time, but we've been in a privileged position to be able to do our jobs. The job that I love.

With Cleland initially acting as caretaker manager, Craig, Callum Booth and Chris Kane had penned six-month deals in May, giving the trio a degree of security in a hugely uncertain period. Club stalwart Murray Davidson, going into his testimonial year, also secured his future. Drey Wright, meanwhile, exited to Hibs.

Liam Craig
It was an extremely tough time, and being PFA Scotland Chairman, I really got to see the ins and outs of just how difficult it was for clubs, and for players. The good thing at St Johnstone was that we had a support network there and a pretty stable, well-run club. We had really good dialogue with the club the whole time. Myself and Jason had numerous Zoom calls with Kirsten (Robertson), who was Head of Football Operations at the time; the Chairman was involved in a few of them as well. You've got to remember, for St Johnstone players, we didn't have a manager either! Tommy had left, but what Jason, being a young captain, has done off the park that people won't see, has been incredible. It's been such a tough time for everyone and for him to steer us through it has been great.

Jason Kerr
It was July 2019 when Tommy gave me the captaincy. We were in pre-season, over in Northern Ireland, and Joe (Shaughnessy) had left at that point, so we hadn't a clue who was going to be the captain. I really didn't expect to be the captain, either. I thought

it might have been maybe Liam Craig or Richard Foster. Tommy told me he wanted to speak to me, and I was, 'Oh, no, what have I done? Am I not fit enough or was my eye off it?' He sat me down and I was a bit nervous, and he goes, 'I want you to be the captain,' and I was like, 'Oh,' just a bit shocked and taken aback.

Mind you, when I did get the captaincy, the first six months of the season didn't really go to plan. I think some of the fans were wanting me out; they wanted somebody else as captain!

But, overall, it's been great. Liam and Richard at the time were both vice, and then it's obviously been Liam ever since and he helped me massively. Honestly, he's got so much experience in the game, he was my right-hand man. He's better at all the backroom work, like talking with the Chairman and all that kind of stuff. There are also other players in the squad, like David Wotherspoon, who have got a lot of experience, and they helped me massively as well. It's a really good group of boys, so they made it really easy for me.

Liam Craig

I signed that six-month contract when we didn't have a manager. And, I'll be honest, at that time, I was looking at it and thinking, 'is this a good time to maybe try and be part of the coaching staff, moving forward?'

Mid-January was when the contract ran out, but I did feel like one of the lucky ones because so many of the players weren't going to get a contract. So to have a six-month contract wasn't ideal, but at least it gave me six months to see what was going to happen, off the park and on the park. Then, a few weeks later, Callum came in, someone I've been close to for a number of years now, and he brought in Steven MacLean.

Fair play to Callum (Booth), and 'Kano' (Chris Kane) as well. They're obviously a wee bit younger than me, so it was probably a difficult decision for them because they might have had even a year's contract from someone else. It might have been easier for them to go and take that, whereas for me, I would never have left as long as there was something there. That's just because of the relationship I've built up with the club over the years, going back to first coming on loan in 2007-8 and winning the First Division in 2009.

Wright had left a core group of players, and notably reduced the average age of the squad, but Davidson was quick to put his own stamp on the group. Isaac Olaofe and Danny McNamara were his first signings, both on loan, having worked with them at Millwall, while Rooney settled in after his move from Inverness. The experienced pair of Craig Conway and then Craig Bryson also arrived.

Danny McNamara, Defender, 22

The loan move worked out great for me. I had come into Millwall for pre-season hoping to be around the first team and push for a start. But the gaffer thought another loan would do me the world of good. I jumped at the chance to come to St Johnstone when it was mentioned. I have to be honest and admit I didn't know much about the club, but Callum was the manager and that was a big attraction. It was a no-brainer for me.

It was a bit nerve wracking when I first went up to Perth. You worry about not making an impact and you could end up sitting on the bench. But it's a great dressing room – definitely one of the best – and I settled right in.

Shaun Rooney, Defender, 25

When Tommy did leave, I thought, 'he must be getting the Northern Ireland job,' and he didn't know who was coming in next. There was a wee bit of uncertainty and then the gaffer got it and he phoned me, probably a week after his arrival, to just say, 'Listen, just come in, work hard and we'll see how things go.' He brought in Danny 'Mac' when I got injured with my ankle in pre-season, and obviously Danny did well and I had to bide my time.

It was great to finally come in after previously agreeing the pre-contract. My great-uncle, Benny, played for Saints, including the League Cup Final in 1969. My dad always said he was manager at Morton and I actually never knew he played here until I signed. My dad said, 'Oh, your great-uncle Benny played for St Johnstone as well,' and I was like, 'Oh, did he?' It's a wee bit of history. That was good, obviously, to have that sort of hanging there, the link with the family.

Jamie McCart

It was a nice move for myself and Shaun. We were sharing a flat in the Highlands and kind of heard at the exact same time from Tommy. He phoned the two of us, one after the other. It was funny. It was brilliant when we both found out and we were eager to come.

St Johnstone historically have been at the top in recent times. They've done brilliantly finishing third, fourth, fifth. You would say they were arguably a top-six club under Tommy, so it was a no-brainer move. I obviously played for a short period and then Covid hit.

That was always the challenge when I signed, to try and get in and impress and show what I could do. It just so happened that in my first game in January 2020, it was the best Celtic have ever played, and they were 3-0 up at Perth after 26 minutes. Since then, I'd like to think I haven't looked back.

Craig Conway, Midfielder, 36

The lads would wind me up about playing for Scotland with the gaffer, but we were a year or two apart in the national squads. Yet he definitely played a huge role in my decision to sign for St Johnstone after being down south for so long. I was impressed with the way he spoke about the club. He was a genuine, nice guy and really he sold it to me. The gaffer also understood my position with living down south and having two young kids.

Obviously, things were difficult for everybody with the pandemic, but he said he could accommodate that and throughout the season I got an extra few days off here and there.

Craig Bryson, Midfielder, 34

I didn't have a good time up at Aberdeen due to injuries. I got an ankle injury that I basically just couldn't get rid of. The gaffer kind of took a chance on me bringing me in, but he gave me a chance to get fit and looked after me. I didn't do every single training session but I was fit for basically every game, except one. It's all credit to him for the way he has managed me.

At Aberdeen, I think it was about 16-18 months that I struggled with the injury. I did a lot of work on the bike and a lot of gym work that nobody sees. I had a lot of lonely times, trying to work as hard as possible. There were some times when I thought, 'is it worth it?' I feel I've had a good career, and maybe this was my body saying 'enough is enough'. I think I was probably getting to a stage where I was going to give it another few months, and if I was still in the same situation, then I would have probably hung up my boots, to be honest. But throughout my whole life and career I've fought to be where I've been, always worked hard, and I always wanted the chance to say 'I'm retiring' rather than my body choosing when I retire. I managed to find a solution, finding this manager and team. I think the work I did stood me in good stead to play the way I have at St Johnstone and be fit.

With experience added to an exciting crop of young players – with the likes of Kerr, Gordon and McCann enjoying successful loan spells and then establishing themselves in the first team – the McDiarmid Park squad had an exciting balance.

Alex Cleland

My first group of young players in 2009 included Stevie May and Zander Clark, when they came in as young 17-year-olds. Derek (McInnes) had said to me, 'We need a full-time coach, Alex, to take over the Under-19s'. I'd just left Inverness as they'd gone down, and St Johnstone had gone up. To see these players still here, and guys like Liam and 'Spoony' (David Wotherspoon), is just great. Others have come through the academy, like Jason Kerr and Chris Kane. They have been on a journey and to see the contribution they are making to the club, they can feel immensely proud.

Davidson, the left-back who came onto the Perth books in 1994 and went on to win 19 Scotland caps, knew all about youth development.

Callum Davidson

I think continuity was a big thing for me. I knew the players. I had worked with a lot of the younger ones coming through, like Jason and Ali. There were a lot of players I had worked with, and got on well with in my time, so I think continuity made it a little bit easier for me. I felt really comfortable coming in. I wasn't unsure of where we were, I knew exactly what I wanted to do. The Chairman is loyal to his managers too. He looks after them and is actually brilliant when you are struggling. It was an easy thing for me to transition into, from assistant to manager at the club. I'm probably glad I left for a couple of years so I could come back fresh.

If Wright's teams were renowned for solidity, led by an experienced, determined defensive core who were hard to beat, Davidson sought to build on his varied learnings to develop a new Perth philosophy. Settling on a back three with flying wing-backs, it was a new style of football for both fans and players to acquaint themselves with – and relish.

Paul Mathers

When Callum came in, who I had worked with before, you always knew he was a studier. He studied everything. Having been away, he brought a freshness from what he had learnt back to the club. Callum loved being on the pitch, working on tactics, and that is probably the one thing he changed just that wee bit. Callum goes into small, small details. He really plans out what he wants to do on a Saturday. How it has fallen into place is amazing. Callum's detail on how we defend and how we attack has been superb.

Callum Davidson

It is probably what I learnt when I was away, learning what the trends and styles were. I love German football. I look a lot at German football and they play 3-4-3 or 5-2-3, whatever you want to call it. They have certain styles of players stepping in. With Gary and Joe at Millwall, we studied that quite a lot. Borussia Dortmund used to play it all the time, Bayern Munich played it as well at times. Germany played that way in the Euros (2020), so did the Italians and so did the Belgians. I looked at those styles – I really liked the fluidity and how easily you could get into good positions. When I looked at the three centre-halves I had, it became an easy choice. With (Scott) Tanser and Booth attacking players, and obviously Danny 'Mac' and Shaun fitting the bill on the other side, I had options.

I watched all the games back from the previous year, where they played a back four quite a lot, and a back three at times. It is credit to Tommy for taking players in like Jamie McCart – he was really good at that and I look to replicate that. To be honest, Shaun struggled a little bit to start with, but all credit to him, he started to listen and I think we found the right system for him to play in.

Steven MacLean

It's not only German football with Callum, we just talk football in general. It's funny. Some days in the office we will start talking and then you look at your watch and go 'wow, is that the time?' Time just sort of passes! He loves the way the German teams have played and different formations, and the fitness in the teams as well. The way they press and work. He always tries to learn. He is always testing me, and I try and fire back questions at him as well. It's about trying to improve; we always try to get better.

It's important too that I'm not just caught up in the game, kicking every ball, but that I take a step back and think about what is going on, and if we need to change it, or tweak it, through speaking to Callum. You have to try and stay calm and focused.

McNamara made his debut on the opening day at newly-promoted Dundee United, with Elliott Parish playing the first eight games in nets due to Zander Clark's knee injury. Ten-man Saints fought back for a point at Tannadice thanks to Liam Craig's sweet volley, displaying a belief and fight that would serve them well.

Craig Conway

I think it was written in the stars that my debut would be at Tannadice (second-half substitute). I wasn't really ready to start the game to be honest, because I had only been in four or five days. I had missed the pre-season.

It would have meant a lot to me if there had been fans in the ground because I had fond memories of my time at United, especially winning the Scottish Cup (in 2010). It felt strange going back there and playing in the opposite side. I would probably have been on remote control and heading for the home dressing room if we hadn't been getting changed under the stand!

Callum Booth, Defender, 30

I'd never worked with the gaffer and I remember I hadn't actually played much in pre-season due to a couple of niggles, and because of Covid there weren't actually that many friendlies. But it was good to start the first league game, and then after that it was kind of chopping and changing a little, before Tanser got a run in the team, which was kind of fair enough as he was playing quite well.

Liam Craig

That performance at Tannadice, especially in the second half, probably epitomised so many performances over the year: down to 10 men, with Mikey (O'Halloran) getting sent off. We're a goal down, we're going up the slope, Dundee United are buzzing, they've just come back into the Premiership and we earn a point.

David Wotherspoon

Liam is a massive influence on anybody. He has got such a great work ethic, is a great lad and his left foot is tremendous. For his age, he is one of the fittest boys I know. He will run all day. Touch wood, he never has that many injuries and is always available. He is an incredible guy to have around the changing room and around the pitch. He is vice captain and leads.

While O'Halloran atoned for his red with a late winner at Kilmarnock, it was a rare highlight in a tricky opening spell for Davidson's men to early October. Indeed, Saints would lose seven of their opening 10 games. With May and Kane absent with injuries, the same spell also only yielded four goals. A mixture of ill-fortune, refereeing decisions and not quite clicking in front of goal caused some head scratching. The late 1-0 back-to-back home defeats to Aberdeen and Hibs in August were particularly sore, with Craig seeing red in the latter. MacLean was even asked if his boots were coming back on . . .

Steven MacLean
It wasn't the greatest start. People probably thought St Johnstone were going to struggle after Tommy left, and it was always going to be difficult. We actually played really well.

Liam Craig
'Cal' (Hendry) scored in the first half against Hibs and got ruled offside – he was onside. It was then the softest penalty with the last kick of the ball, that was the frustration.

People laugh at this, but I get on great with the referees. You know, Craig Thomson stays just along the road from me. Some Saturday nights, if I'd go down to the Chinese or a takeaway, I'd see him, and we would talk about his game and talk about my game, or who was refereeing a game and talk about different decisions. If I'd see him out at the nursery or the school, I'd talk to him.

David Wotherspoon
If you look back at the results, it was 1-0 defeats here and there. I felt our performances were decent. We just couldn't quite get over the line with wins. We definitely believed if we kept plugging away it would work, while the transition of the new manager and new system we were playing was always going to take a wee bit of time. We all believed it would turn for us. We had a great squad there, so we just needed the belief to try and turn it round.

Chris Kane
I got a wee injury at the start of the season so that set me back a bit. I was in pre-season and my calf went. Sitting watching the games was frustrating, but you could obviously see the performances were there. The manager kept on saying that. They were creating chances, but they just couldn't put the ball away, so

that was the most frustrating part: playing well but not actually getting the goals and the results. That was obviously annoying for me, but I just had to focus on getting my calf better and getting back on the training pitch.

Michael O'Halloran, Forward, 30

I felt we were playing some good football, bedding into the new system. I think maybe it was just that bit of confidence we were missing and getting on a run.

Callum Hendry, Forward, 23

It was one of those things that, as a striker, sometimes you're just not finding the back of the net. It happens to everyone. And that was us. At the start of the season, the gaffer came in and we were still trying to find how we wanted to play. We were getting to grips with everything, it was completely new.

Craig Conway

Even when things weren't going too great at the start, the gaffer stuck to his guns. I really respected that. The gaffer wasn't one of those who would change things dramatically because the wins weren't coming.

Jason Kerr

We put a lot of hard work in and did a lot of work on shape in training. It was obviously never going to gel straight away at the start of the season. It would have been hard for the gaffer to come in and get us to play a certain way straight away and win games, so it might have taken us a few months before we managed to show how good we are at that formation. I'm glad the gaffer was really patient, because I think any other manager, under the pressure, probably would have changed it, and changed it for good. I'm really glad that he managed to keep it the same formation. I feel that we had a really good understanding as a back three, myself, Liam and Jamie. I've also known Liam for a while. I've played with him at youth level, and I've played against him too.

Liam Gordon

I know we weren't getting results, but I always felt the performances were there and I was always confident that this team was going to turn round. We obviously just chose to do it at the best point in time.

Jason Kerr

I don't think we were playing badly at the start of the season. I think people looking at the results would think, 'oh, well, they must be playing really poorly,' but we were playing really good football.

McNamara's cross balls, in particular, were a highlight of Saints' attacking play, but nobody was really getting on the end of the deliveries.

Danny McNamara

I was more used to a back four than playing wing-back. Every game I was learning more and more. You have to put in a shift but I loved it. I was getting regular football at a very good standard. Some people down in England don't give Scottish football the respect it deserves. I came up against some very good players, guys like Borna Barisic and Ryan Kent at Rangers.

Off the field, the fans were great and so friendly – and my neighbours couldn't have done more for me. They let me use their parking space and sometimes I would get a knock on the door and they would be giving me something for dinner! I was so lucky. They looked after me.

Shaun Rooney

Obviously, it was tough at the start, but you've just got to bide your time. I've always believed in myself, there's no point in playing football if you don't believe in your abilities, so I always knew if I did the right things and bided my time, I would have my chance.

With goals in short supply, Parish was short on luck at the other end too.

Zander Clark, Goalkeeper, 29

Watching the games from the stand it was like 'how are we not three or four up?' We were creating so many chances and you could see we were a good team. It was a sort of a travesty how we didn't pick up more points with the performances we were putting in. Things weren't falling for us and we were getting punished for a wee lapse in concentration. We knew we weren't far away. 'El' (Elliott Parish) was excellent for us. His performances deserved so many more clean sheets than he got.

Paul Mathers

You look to pair up the squad. We had seen Elliott at Dundee and we felt he would be a good fit. He was lively and bubbly. He has come in and supported Zander and the two young goalkeepers, Ross Sinclair and Jack Wills, and done incredibly well at that. People forget he did well for those eight games, the matches at Tannadice, Rugby Park and against Hibs and Aberdeen at McDiarmid. I think that gave him a big lift, to be able to show his worth. He is great about the place, trains hard, is bubbly, and loud – very loud at times. He supports the keepers and the players week-in, week-out. He is a capable goalkeeper to come in and play in his own right, which is perfect for the manager. It does help that he is experienced.

Elliott Parish, Goalkeeper, 31

The start of the season we just couldn't score a goal. We lost a lot of games 1-0. We won 2-1 at Kilmarnock, but we were 1-0 down for the most part. At any level, we weren't clinical at that stage of the season.

I try to be solid, do the basics and make the odd good save, which is, I guess, how I was playing. But it's irrelevant, if you are, as I am at the club, the No. 2 keeper. When you play, if the results don't go your way you will be out of that side. As reliant as I was on my own performances, the team needed to be winning games to keep the shirt off Zander which takes some doing. The problem was we weren't picking up results.

Liam Craig

Ten games into the season, it's not great in terms of results, but you're looking at it, and you're going, 'Guy (Melamed) wasn't here, 'Mayso' (Stevie May) was injured, Kano was injured, Zander was injured.' People forget those four key players throughout the season were missing at that point, while Muzz (Murray Davidson) missed the start of the season too.

But in training there was never, ever a negative atmosphere. From the manager down, everything was positive, and everyone was enjoying it. Maybe I'm just getting old, but I enjoy my football more now than I've ever done, even at the start of the season. With the manager coming in, I loved him as a coach and as a player, especially his enthusiasm. That's why he was so successful with Tommy, so successful with Scotland. Alright, Stoke maybe didn't work out, but you see how successful he was at Millwall as well, and it's just that infectious enthusiasm that he brings – not just to football, you see what he's like in every sport. That rubs off on the players when you're coming into work every day.

Craig Bryson

When I came in there was no panic. I think when I signed in September we were almost bottom of the league. I was sitting in the stand for the first couple of games, or on the bench, and I was thinking 'we are actually playing some really good football here.' We just weren't taking chances or were getting hit on the sucker punch. The gaffer kept saying the same things. He couldn't fault us, we just needed to be more clinical as a team. He stuck to his guns, our training never changed, our game plans never changed. No matter how many changes the gaffer made, we still played the same way. Everybody knew their job in the team and that's testament to the work we did on the training ground.

Of the various key points in the season, 26 September 2020 at Livingston was among the most notable. Saints, playing a flat back four, were off the pace and 2-0 losers in West Lothian after the concession of two quick-fire first-half goals.

Liam Gordon

The manager filled me in on the Friday and said that he was going for the formation – but he wasn't going to play me. As a manager, I always respect his decisions, so I was like, 'right, whatever, I can deal with that.' And then the game didn't pan out. I don't really think it was just down to the formation, but I do feel that when you have three centre-halves across the pitch, you're going to have a better chance to win a game of football. We spoke after the match, and I think he realised that. We went through a phase where we weren't scoring, weren't picking up points, and he just said to me, 'look, it's got nothing to do with your performance, I just feel I have to change something as manager,' and I fully respected him for that. That's just football at the end of the day. You're a team: if you think that it's going to benefit the team, you just take it on the chin.

Steven MacLean

For me, we went to Livingston, changed our system and lost 2-0. Afterwards we spoke about it, and Callum said, 'No, we'll stick to what we've done (previously, i.e. play with three centre-halves) and we'll get better at it and we'll improve.' We had done well; we just weren't taking chances or having the rub of the green. That would maybe be a turning point in the season. Callum stuck to what he believed in and we went with it.

Jamie McCart

I think the three centre-halves works well for the team. With the two wing-backs, if it is Shaun and Callum, they go up and down, are good going forward but they'll get back too. Either side of the defence, myself and Jason are comfortable going out in areas with the ball and without, and then you've obviously got Gordon in the middle, who's like an organiser, he's perfect. I mean, when you watch a game, all you can hear is Gordon on the TV! I think the best word is we 'complement' each other so well.

Callum Davidson

The only thing that worried me was that we were playing so well, we were getting that many opportunities and we weren't taking them. I remember saying to 'Macca' and Alex 'I'm coming off the pitch with the same conversation.' It was killing me. Thankfully I don't follow Twitter.

I was racking my brain, 'what do I do?' I phoned a couple of people for advice (Gary Rowett and ex-team-mate Graham Alexander). One person said do one thing and the other person said do the other, so it didn't really help! One said change it and one said stick to your beliefs. I think probably the best thing that happened was that we played terribly at Livingston with a back four, if that makes sense. I'd thought, 'I'm going to change it.

I'm going to play 4-2-3-1 against Livi'. And we were poor, really poor. At that point, I thought 'C'mon Cal, we're good at what we're doing' and it definitely turned.

The Chairman could have been sitting there questioning himself, but at that point he was brilliant with me. He said, 'listen Cal, your football is brilliant, what you are doing, what you are trying to do, we've got a certain style of how we are playing, stick at it, keep going and it will turn for you'. For me, that is probably the biggest endorsement I can give him, as how he backed me at that point. That home game against Hibs we probably scored a goal (from Hendry) that wasn't offside, so the breaks weren't coming either. I remember going home to Lorna (my wife) and saying 'I would rather be a lucky manager, than a good manager'. But she basically told me to be quiet, shut up and get on with it. At that point, I was really thinking 'what am I doing wrong?' But as we know things can change and we stuck to our beliefs. That probably went through the team for the rest of the season.

On Sunday 4 October, Saints again earned plaudits but no points in a 2-0 home defeat to champions Celtic. The away strikes came in the 90th minute and beyond. Resultantly, Saints fell to the foot of the table on goal difference below St Mirren. They had seven points from 10 games.

'Yet this was a performance that offered encouragement for St Johnstone,' read the BBC Scotland online match report. 'Though they have been on a poor run, they looked confident on the ball and assured in their defending, with the back three especially impressive. With better finishing, they could have won the game.'

Stevie May
It was frustrating, but the manager was good. He looked at all the stats that compared us to other teams in the league, like the

chances we were creating. It was kind of just showing us we were playing good football and if we stuck to it, then, you know, the odds say it's got to turn at some point and get going in your favour. And it did in the end.

THREE

BUILDING BLOCKS

'I'll follow the Saints through the glory and the strife,
our love is unrestricted'
'Fair Maid'
The Shrugs
(2014 Scottish Cup Final Song)

*If Scotland's nerve-shredding Euro 2020 play-off semi-final against
Israel – eventually won on penalties – dominated the football
headlines in early October 2020, the international break was to
ultimately have a significant impact on Saints' fortunes. Betfred
League Cup ties against Kelty Hearts and Brechin, as well as the
league match at Hamilton after the break, may seem unlikely
occasions to kick-start a season – but how important the contests
proved to be.*

Callum Davidson
I quite like the format of the Betfred Cup in the international
break. What it does is give you the chance to play other players.
My squad was compact and it basically gave me the opportunity
to play everyone, so everyone was part of the team.

Jason Kerr

I feel like the gaffer stuck to the game plan that we had. Even after the 10 games where we weren't doing so well, we had a system. He wanted to stick to that, and fair play to him, because eventually it turned out so well for us, and we played really good football.

Liam Gordon

It started to gel and it came from the hard work on the training ground, a lot of shape, and that's not just from the three of us as defenders (Gordon, Kerr and McCart), it's filtered through the whole team. You see how well Booth and Wotherspoon link on the left-hand side, you have Rooney, the strikers and then you've got the likes of McCann, Davidson and Bryson in the middle as well. Everyone just knows their job and it's just engrained in us.

Jason Kerr

At the time, we weren't thinking, 'Oh, this is going to be a good cup run.' We were actually thinking, 'We need to get our finger out or we're going to get humiliated here (in the league).' We needed to start picking up points in the league. So initially, that was the aim, just to start doing well in the league; we weren't even thinking of the cup competition. So, it was good that we did obviously change it in that sense.

We hadn't scored many goals at all. So, with all respect to Kelty, just to get my first goal since I scored against Hibs at Easter Road in August 2019 was a bit of a relief on a personal note (netting at the end of the first half). It could have been quite an awkward game for us if Kelty had scored the first goal, because Kelty's a tough place to play. We were professional and got the job done. Kano scored in that game as well. It was good to get to play in cup games, it was a bit of a distraction from the league. That's where the journey started, isn't it?

Scott Tanser, Defender, 26

I remember the game against Kelty Hearts in the group stages only too well. We knew it would be a tough one because they would want to make a name for themselves.

They were kicking anything that moved that night. Let's just say it was an experience! It was very difficult to get our game going. But we got a 2-0 lead and even though they got one back we finished quite comfortably.

After winning at Kelty, seven further goals followed at home to Brechin. May (hat-trick), Wotherspoon (double), Hendry and Davidson found the net. Belief grew.

David Wotherspoon

It was funny, as everyone was talking about how we weren't scoring goals but all of a sudden we got a few and then we just couldn't stop scoring. I think that was the sort of turning point for our season, getting those goals and the confidence in our team to go and win games.

Stevie May

Yeah, I think the turning point was probably the Betfred Cup games, we scored a few goals in the games like against Brechin. That was a big game for us.

Davidson and MacLean were encouraging May – who returned to the club in 2019 – to regain his predatory instincts from his dream 2013-14 season, to be unselfish and do his best work inside the penalty area.

Stevie May

It's a lot different in many ways now to 2014, obviously personnel and players have changed, even if some players and coaches were here first time round. Personally, looking back, I probably didn't even make the right decisions half the time. Sometimes it was fine, other times I was very raw in what I was doing.

I wouldn't have been as comfortable taking the ball and picking the right options, so to speak. Like, sometimes I see options now which I wouldn't have seen back in the day, like a pass that's on or something like that, so it's kind of good and bad: now I'll see things that I wouldn't have seen then, but back then I would have just had a shot and I might have been shouted at by half the team!

I kind of want to try to go back to that, but if there's a better option, I try and use that. I mean, whatever we did as a squad last season seemed to work, so it just shows that being selfish all the time maybe isn't beneficial.

Alistair Stevenson, Head of Youth Academy

When I left for Hibs, Stevie was the youngest player in the academy at that time, 11 or 12. I spotted him. He was pointed out to me playing with the community department. He was with Atholl Henderson's group. I said to Atholl one morning when I was watching, 'Who is the wee boy with the yellow T-shirt?' He said, 'That's Stevie May from Newburgh, he is a good player eh?' I said, 'Yeah, he looks terrific.' He started to come in and train. At that point, he was a wee midfielder and I went away and moved on to Hibs.

I noticed he started to develop as a striker, somebody saw a real talent there. He got his breakthrough quite quickly. He went on loan and got better and better. It came to the 2014 cup run and he was on fire. He got moves down south and to Aberdeen, had a couple of injuries, but he is back to being fit and healthy. I think he would have played a lot more last season if it hadn't been for the fact Chris (Kane) was playing so well.

Callum Hendry

I was enjoying it. Beating Brechin at home, which I scored in, was a big positive. It was the start of the cup runs and I was delighted to be a part of that.

Michael O'Halloran

The League (Betfred) Cup I think helped in terms of confidence. That drove us on. We were playing some really nice football; we just weren't scoring enough, and luckily for us the tide turned. We knew ourselves we were playing well and we were doing everything right.

Steven MacLean

I think we just had to keep believing and playing well. I think the Betfred Cup helped us, as we got a bit of momentum, scored some goals and the boys got confidence from that. From there, I think we took off a little.

Paul Mathers

I know we were in a bubble and it was time consuming, but having the Betfred in the international breaks of October and November worked quite well. We started scoring goals and it kick-started us. The games were pretty constant and we were in that mode for the whole season, as such.

Stevie May

Then we took it into the next game and scored five as a team at Hamilton, when we hadn't been scoring goals at all, and it gave us that further confidence boost.

After a crazy 5-3 win in South Lanarkshire, with May grabbing a brace, Davidson's men had suddenly netted 14 goals in three games. What striking problems?

David Wotherspoon

Craig Conway played a massive part, especially at the start of the season. He was in and out, but whenever he was needed or expected to play, he performed at the very high level that he is renowned for in his career. He is a top-level player. His delivery at set pieces was incredible to watch. You just have to look at that goal at Hamilton to see his ability. He put it right in the top corner when we were winning 4-3 to secure the win.

Craig Conway

That was a mad, mad game. We were up 3-0 but let them back into it. It was to and fro in the closing stages. I had a few chances in games leading up to that one and I was just relieved to get off the mark.

My second one was a free-kick. I had made up my mind I would go to the goalkeeper's side and I don't think I could have hit it any sweeter if I'd tried 100 times. I had taken free-kicks at previous clubs but there was usually someone ahead of me that was slightly better at them. I remember one for Dundee United against Hearts that was a bit further out and I put it into the top corner. It was brilliant to be fair. But the goal against Accies was right up there – and it was such an important goal for us.

We badly needed the three points that day. It was all very well playing well, but I felt we were banging the same drum, playing well without the results to go with it. We didn't know how the season was going to shape up. Were we going to be involved in a relegation battle?

I have played under managers who went back to basics and tried to scrap wins. So, hats off to the gaffer for having the confidence and belief to stick with it. It ended up paying dividends.

Danny McNamara

I was gutted no fans were there at the games. You want to play in front of your supporters. I would have loved them to have been there when I finally scored for St Johnstone – it was the winner against Kilmarnock in November.

I could have scored four or five times before that and I was getting a bit of stick for not hitting the target. It was a huge relief – and a proud moment for me. My family watched all the games on SaintsTV. It was such a shame they weren't there for that moment.

Scott Tanser

I missed a penalty in the penalty shoot-out against Dundee United in the Betfred Cup, but we felt the 0-0 draw would be enough for us, going up to Peterhead for the next one.

5 October 2020: Newsflash . . .

'St Johnstone have signed forward Guy Melamed from Maccabi Netanya. Melamed has scored 50 goals in 178 club appearances and helped Hapoel Beer Sheva win the Israeli Premier League in 2018.' (BBC online)

After a 40-day wait – including 14 days of isolation – the Balmoor Stadium at Peterhead was the unlikely setting for Saints' new striker to have his baptism.

Guy Melamed, Forward, 28

It was tough for many reasons. Because of the virus, my friends and family couldn't see me and I had to self-isolate in the hotel after I signed for the club. I had no normal life outside football so I only saw Scotland through a bus window going to matches. That was very disappointing.

It was the first time I had played with a club outside my own country and it was a very difficult few months for me. After arriving, I had to try to stay fit in the hotel room. It is hard, mentally, getting out of bed and doing exercises in a bedroom.

I couldn't even go out so the club arranged for an exercise bike and that helped me before I could train with the players. From the professional side I had to get used to a very different style of football from what I was used to in Israel. I had heard so much about the culture of the Scottish supporters, how they sing and cheer during games. I feel disappointed to have missed out on that experience.

Peterhead was definitely a culture shock for me. It was challenging. I knew it wasn't going to be an example for the Premiership and I had played against smaller teams in Israel in cups. But the weather was so different from what I was used to at home. It was no fun! The ground is on the coast. I couldn't believe it was so cold and windy. It was meant to be summer! The gaffer told me after the game not to worry. It wouldn't always be like that, thank goodness.

Of course, I had incredibly met Liam Gordon and Callum Hendry on holiday in Miami. My agent reminded me of that after I had signed. They had mentioned it to the gaffer. I did remember meeting Scottish players and we had talked about football, Miami and Israel. But who could imagine two years later we would be in the same team? It is such a small world.

It was to be January before Melamed netted, but it was worth the wait for the Perth boss.

Callum Davidson

Anybody coming in from a different country, a different style of football, a different way of life can find it hard. One problem was Guy had to isolate for 14 days when he came in. The poor lad was stuck in a place on his own. It took him time. We could see glimpses of him being good, but we knew he wasn't fit enough and he had to work harder.

I think it was hard for him and it was difficult for me

because he was kind of like a bit of a marquee signing for me. I just believed it was the right thing. I think Guy was getting frustrated. His agent was phoning me in January saying, 'Can he leave, can he leave?' I said, 'No, I'm going to give him a chance'. I had made the decision to let Callum (Hendry) go (on loan to Aberdeen at the end of January). As a management decision it's not great when you let a striker go to another team in the league, but I believed Callum had to go and play a lot of games and score goals. That left me an area to put Guy in the team. I am pretty strong in what I believe in, I won't be swayed by what people say or I can hear in the press, or wherever. I really stick to my guns. I will always do it. It's my decision, nobody else's.

Liam Gordon
Come the new year, Guy scored big goals.

Meantime, May's purple patch of eight goals in seven games helped ease Saints into the last-16 of the Betfred League Cup with the win at Peterhead. An entertaining 2-2 draw on league business at Hibs offered further optimism, with McCann netting and continuing to shine in midfield.

David Wotherspoon
It's just amazing to see where Ali has come from. At the start of 2019 he went to Stranraer on loan and he has developed from there. I was travelling with him every day to training and listened to him speaking about how he was happy playing every week, getting experience and really enjoying it. To come back, put in the pre-season he did, then start playing games, it's been incredible to see where he is. He deserves everything he is getting. He works so hard, is a level-headed young boy and he is always happy. He is never stroppy, always looking on the positive side of things. Just to see where he has got to now, playing international football for

Northern Ireland, a main part of our team, he is just a joy to watch sometimes. The way he can break up play with ease, he makes it look so easy to make a tackle or get the ball back.

Ali McCann, Midfielder, 21

It's maybe pot luck with my positional sense for 50-50 balls and hopefully it carries on! The systems we played last year, you have to get the hang of where to play, sitting back or going forward and I cover a lot of ground which lends itself to my game really. But the experienced players help as well as they gave me advice on where to go, who to pick up and to make runs forward as and when.

They are like an insurance policy, sweeping everything up. Liam (Craig) seems to be getting better anyway, it gave me that extra freedom to help me express myself alongside him. But whoever was beside me I could rely on.

David Wotherspoon

It was just a pleasure to watch Ali and play alongside him. He has great ability and talent to progress in football. I really enjoy playing with him. Alex Ferguson is a talented young footballer as well at the club, has great composure on the ball for his age, and I'm really excited at the prospect of him progressing as well. He is a joy to watch, too.

Wotherspoon himself was starting to play some of the best football of his career, also chipping in with six goals by the end of November in a free role allowing the now Canadian internationalist to take responsibility, roam and create.

David Wotherspoon

Even when Callum was the assistant, he always said he liked me playing centrally. Since he came, that is what he said again.

Even though I might be up front on the left or left of midfield, I'm still coming in and trying to play in the middle of the park, trying to provide and create for the team. I've just really enjoyed the role, because I've got that freedom with players behind me that can do the dirty side of the work and let me sort of express myself going forward. It just makes my life easier when you've got those players providing balls into me, or making runs to let me get on the ball. I feel like the fact I'm 31 now there is a bit more responsibility on me. I feel the gaffer gave me that by selecting me in starting XIs quite a lot of the season. I hope I can help and provide for others around me as well.

Successful seasons hinge on defining moments and Wotherspoon was at the centre of a stunning 2-1 comeback triumph at Motherwell to seal a Betfred Cup quarter-final place. O'Halloran's lightning pace was also instrumental in hauling Saints off the canvas.

David Wotherspoon

It was a huge game. They were in a bit of form at that point and we were still a little inconsistent. We knew if we dug in we could get back in the game. We got the equaliser, when Callum (Hendry) scored, from Michael's great work down the wing. The winner came through Michael again, sheer determination down the line, not giving up on the ball, and he managed to get the ball into the box and luckily I managed to get a good touch on it and put it in at the front post. I was delighted, absolutely buzzing. I was on a good run of scoring too at that point. It was a massive result and we were on our way in the League Cup.

Callum Hendry

Mikey was unbelievable in that game. If he uses his pace, you can't live with it, because he's the fastest boy in the league by a country mile. He was just running and running down the wing, and I know I scored, but he made it easy for me. So, I'll take the credit for the goal, but a lot of it has to go to him as well for the way he played in that game, for both goals. It was an unbelievable touch from Spoony, such a hard angle. Little moments can change everything. Crazy, isn't it?

David Wotherspoon

I was getting interviews at that point and I was on six goals, scoring and setting up others. I really wanted to add to that. It seems to happen every time I get those interviews and they ask me 'how many goals do you want to score this season?' As soon as I say a number, I don't seem to score after that! I didn't score from then on, which I was gutted about, but the main thing is I felt like I played a major part in helping the team to its success.

Michael O'Halloran

I thought we actually played quite well at Fir Park, and then we lost a goal just after the hour, I would say against the run of play. There were a couple of really good moves, and we just didn't get on the end of them. I felt confident, even going behind, that we were going to score anyway. It was pleasing for me that I got two assists. I remember the first one – Cal did really well and it came back off the goalie. And then 'D' (Wotherspoon) as well, for the second one, he made a great run across the front post. Two really good finishes got us to the next round.

I was 30 in January, but there are players older than me still performing going forward. Look at Jamie Vardy, for example, and he's still razor-sharp, lightning quick at 34. I look after myself and do extra gym work. But for me, pace is a natural thing. You've either got it or you've not, and I'm lucky enough to have it, but you can always work on it as well. I think there's always room for improvement. I know it's a big asset and it's not really a worry for me, when there are players older than me that are still quick. Don't get me wrong: I will lose it one day, the legs are going to go! But it's not something I'm really too worried about.

The cup was also opening up, offering opportunity. On the same day as Saints won at 'Well, Hearts and Aberdeen exited. Ross County then stunned Celtic, while St Mirren did likewise against Rangers.

Callum Davidson

Obviously, goals came for us and that bred confidence. That was a big win at Motherwell. It was great play from Michael. I thought he was excellent at wing-back that day. It was a big goal from Callum. He kind of lost his confidence a little bit. It was difficult for him as we had Mayso out and Kano out. We were really, really struggling for top end strikers and all the pressure was on Callum.

Jason Kerr

I think we always had that bit of confidence, but we just needed to turn in good performances and get the actual results.

Liam Gordon

The Betfred games were huge for us for our momentum, in terms of just needing someone to put the ball in the net.

Davidson's own patience was also paying off.

Callum Davidson

I looked at stats at that point and for most crosses in the box we were behind Rangers, which was incredible. Shots conceded, one of the least. Everything was there, it was in place. What I did look at was stats on when we conceded goals, from zero to five, from 40 to 45, 45 to 50 and 80 to 90. I put it up on the board and it was incredible, the points we lost with that. I think a lot of lads went 'oh, I can't believe that'. I thought that's not fitness levels, as I looked at all the goals back, it was just concentration and realising where we were in the game. If you look at our record after that, I think that, for me, is the biggest thing as to why we had the success we did. We stopped losing goals at the wrong times, so gave ourselves a chance to win the game or get a result in the game.

Liam Gordon

The manager did that in the video. He sat us down and was just basically saying, 'there's nothing to worry about, we're doing everything right'. I think we'd had the second most crosses and the third most shots in the league so far, and that was like November-time, so it showed we were doing the right things, we just needed to be more clinical.

From early season troubles, Saints had now strung together an 11-game unbeaten run – with only Celtic's late leveller denying a famous win on 6 December after Kane's opener in Glasgow.

Chris Kane

Stevie and I played well together, and then obviously Guy came in and he started scoring goals from January, so he was staying in the team as well. No matter who I played with, I thought we had a good relationship. Obviously, the main thing I've got to do is keep myself in the team, but it's only fair to rotate the squad and keep everyone fresh and fit.

Danny McNamara

We got a good point against Celtic which boosted our confidence. We had chances to win that one. That is some stadium, even when it's empty. It's a shame I didn't get to play in front of big crowds at grounds against Celtic, Rangers and Hibs. I can't even imagine what the atmosphere must be like when they are full.

Yet, all the good work was almost undone in the cup. Saints dominated at Dunfermline in the quarter-final, especially in the first half, but couldn't convert. It was one of those nights. Rooney's strike early in extra time seemed set to settle it, before the Pars forced penalties.

Callum Davidson

I remember speaking to Stevie (Crawford) and Greg (Shields) and they couldn't deal with us in the first half. For a club like St Johnstone to play against a team like that, I was actually really pleased with the first half performance. I thought it was incredible. I played Ali McCann higher up on the right hand side, he played in the front three. He is such an intelligent player, with his movement. We managed to basically boss the game and create chance after chance.

Ali McCann

In the Dunfermline game, and the game at Ibrox in the Scottish Cup quarter-finals, I was part of the front three which was a bit different for me, but I've played there before for Northern Ireland Under-21s. Everyone knows their jobs, about who to pick up and press on.

Steven MacLean

The most nervous I think I've been was the Dunfermline game with the penalties. I remember sitting on the bench thinking 'wow, I don't enjoy this!' We should have been out of sight that night before penalties.

Shaun Rooney

Dunfermline, in the Betfred. We should have won in normal time. Thankfully Zander saved us.

Digging deep, Saints reached the Scottish League Cup semi-finals for the first time since 2016. After Paul Watson and Hendry missed for each side in the shoot-out, Clark saved from Kevin O'Hara to allow Craig to step up and seal the win.

Liam Craig
It was a relief, simple as that.

Zander Clark
It was a massive night. It was a tricky game. We dominated, but couldn't finish it off like games at the start of the season. Going into penalties, you're thinking 'please don't let this come back and bite us'. Thankfully we managed to reach the semi-final.

As a young kid coming through the ranks, I've always had top-class keepers to look up to. Whether it be Alan Main, Peter Enckelman, Alan Mannus or Steve Banks, I've picked up wee traits from each individual and formed myself into a better keeper.

Paul Mathers
When I arrived, Zander was 23 and he had just come back from his second loan spell at Queen of the South. The plan was to then integrate him in the first team and challenge Alan. I had watched him at Queen of the South and also kept a slight eye on him at Elgin and realised he had been sent off a couple of times at Elgin when he was younger. I had an idea of what I wanted to improve.

I saw certain things in Zander's game I looked to change and Tommy was fine with that. I got to know Zander, started slowly, and then began to implement the wee changes. When he did get in the team, and knew what we were looking for, the one thing I noticed straight away was his temperament. It is so good and one of his biggest assets. If he makes a mistake it doesn't bother him and he bounces back.

He is also a big presence in nets for penalties. He is very laid back and he trusts me a lot of the time with the information I give him. Losing to Dundee United on penalties earlier in the Betfred Cup group stage (after the 0-0 draw) was a big disappointment, so when it came to the Dunfermline game we knew the importance. Just getting to know Zander, he is trusting. I trust him and he trusts me, in terms of how we go about the job, the information we give each other and our feedback to each other. I can never remember us locking horns and disagreeing on anything really.

Callum Hendry
It was bittersweet at Dunfermline. I came on and made a difference, played really well, and then I hit the bar on my penalty!

Stevie May
That win was big for us as our motto in terms of the whole season was 'you just keep going, go to the end'. Big games followed, like Hibs in the semi-final, and after that, you just kind of think your name is maybe on this trophy.

Jamie McCart
I think if you look back, even when Celtic and Rangers win trophies, you look at games that they've maybe scraped by, and different things. You probably need wee bits of luck when you're playing maybe six or seven one-off games; you need something to go your way, and it was good for us they did.

Callum Davidson
There are little moments in seasons, it is how you win cups. After we beat Dunfermline, I kind of felt 'oh, we've got a chance'. It keeps the season going, looking forward to a semi-

final at the end of January. I get asked 'what was the biggest win of the season?' But there were lots of big wins that culminated in having the season we did.

With the Hampden last-four tie with Hibs on the back burner, frustrations returned in the league before the New Year. A 3-2 loss at St Mirren when Kerr saw red. A controversial 2-1 defeat at Aberdeen when Hendry saw red. A 0-0 draw at home to Hamilton when Saints had 28 shots. Fans behind TV screens were tearing their hair out, myself included.

Scott Tanser

St Mirren was a setback for us. Jason got red carded in that game. I know the fans were getting a bit worried about a relegation battle when we weren't getting results. That defeat probably didn't make them change their minds. We were still floating around the bottom of the table.

Jason Kerr

Yeah, there was definitely a big disruption in my season because the sending off was a really bad one for me. We were playing well at that point, 2-1 up, and it was near enough half-time, and I just didn't need to step out and make that challenge. I never really dive and all that, so I surprised myself by doing that. It would have been really hard for the boys to hold on to a 2-1 lead and they went on and got beaten late on. It was a tough one for me, and obviously, I apologised to the boys, but I was off with Covid as well.

I had a few of the symptoms. I lost my smell and my taste. I don't actually know where I got it, so it shows just how careful everybody needs to be – wash your hands and wear your mask. It's proof that it can get anyone. But I'm glad the gaffer kept faith in me, I feel like he would've had every right to keep me on the bench, because I wouldn't say I was playing amazingly well at that point. I'm just happy the gaffer kept faith in me and we went on and did so well in the season.

Michael O'Halloran

I remember coming on in that Accies game, and I had a chance as well. If you look at footage of the game, we had more than enough chances to go and score three, four goals or more.

Callum Booth

I had a couple of injuries, so it was a little bit stop-start for me, I suppose. But it was good competition with Scott. I came on for him after five minutes at Aberdeen after his knee injury.

I remember they got a penalty, through (Sam) Cosgrove. It was never a penalty, and we lost 2-1. But, basically, since that game, I think our luck just kind of switched a little bit and we just went on this incredible run.

As the curtain closed on 2020 – a year nobody will ever forget mainly for the wrong reasons – Saints sat ninth in the table, just three points above bottom-placed Accies having played a game more. But all eyes were soon turning to Hibs. With Livingston facing St Mirren in the other semi-final, a golden opportunity lay in wait for all four clubs to try and lift silverware.

Jason Kerr

The worst bit of my time out (from Covid) was having to sit in my house by myself for 10 days doing nothing. I was watching every game and cheering on the boys. It was my first semi-final and I was buzzing to get back for it. I felt we had a squad good enough to go and win the trophy.

FOUR

GOODBYE HAMPDEN HOODOO

'Go on, that's in. That's another goal,
Saints have made it three. Absolutely fantastic.'
Steven Watt, SaintsTV

As 2021 arrived, Saints faced three league games before they could turn their attention to bidding to reach a first League Cup Final since 1998. With McNamara recalled back south to Millwall, James Brown came north from The Den in another loan move until the end of the season.

James Brown, Defender, 23

Danny was the first person I phoned as soon as I got asked towards the back end of December, 'would you like to come up?' I spoke to Danny and I thought, 'yeah, if he's coming back, then I might as well just do a quick swap'. I think I got the better half of the season if I'm totally honest!

I remember the Millwall boys when he came back were just bantering a bit, saying 'he's gone up there and got them half-relegated' because I think Saints were near the bottom at halfway. I came up, we started winning and kicked on.

The boys loved Callum as an assistant at Millwall. When he

left, I think a lot of the boys were sad to see him go. He was good there, like he is now as a manager, no different. You see him now, he's so laid back, which I think is nice – he takes the pressure off you as a player. You go out there, he will tell you what he wants from you, but there's so much relaxation in what you can go and do in your position.

But it's funny. I came up here straight away and the first test we did, I got Covid. So, I had come up, had to isolate in the flat up here and I literally hadn't seen anything. I had literally come up on the Monday morning, come in, positive test, went back to the flat and I was in there for 10 days straight, ordering food online and everything like that. It wasn't the ideal start.

Shaun Rooney
Obviously, big 'Jase' got suspended, so I played a couple of games at centre-half before Danny 'Mac' left. I thought I was playing alright, to be fair, not anything special but was playing alright, and when Danny 'Mac' got recalled, I sort of knew there was a route back into the team. When 'Browny' came in, I always had to just sort of bring my game up, to be fair. It's always good to have that challenge.

Davidson's side went to Dingwall on 2 January but could only return with a point. Saints remained just two points above bottom-placed County.

Craig Conway
I was brought down for the penalty and no one else was getting to take it! Dingwall is a tough place to go but we probably should have won. We had chances to get all three points. I had taken penalties previously, including at Blackburn, so I had no qualms about taking that one.

I always think you have to make your decision early and stick with it. Once before, I changed my mind at the last minute and hit the post. So, I said to myself, 'never again'. You can live with it if you have been outsmarted by a goalkeeper. But changing your mind sticks with you.

Another point followed on the road at Dundee United in an entertaining 2-2 draw, but Saints were now winless in 10 league games, and Clark was beaten by a remarkable 53-yard lob from Lawrence Shankland. It was goal-of-the-season material.

Callum Davidson

I just thought 'wow'. Sometimes you've just got to take your hat off. It was like (Luka) Modric for Croatia against Scotland at the Euros. Sometimes you've just got to stand up and clap. A great bit of skill.

Zander Clark

It was one of them! Sometimes you've just got to tip your hat and say 'brilliant'. I felt I was in a relatively decent position. It's a slack pass inside from us and it just sits up perfectly for him. You could probably go and give him another 50 attempts and he'll not manage to recreate it.

Paul Mathers

If Zander was out of position, maybe too central, it wasn't a disaster. On looking at it, we came to the conclusion pretty quickly from looking at the video after the game, it was just a heck of a finish. The execution was incredible. But Zander's reaction was good, as it didn't get to him. Not a lot fazes him. He probably gets more annoyed day-to-day with his own performances than he does on match days.

Callum Davidson

During the season, I never once felt as though we were in a rut, even when we were bottom of the league. If we were playing badly and losing games, I would have gone 'Oh no, I definitely need something to change'. But not once in the season did I think we were struggling, were poor. Not one team really dominated us. We are trying to play a style of football where we don't allow teams opportunities in our box, try to high press when we can, drop into our shape when we have to and we have a certain discipline on how we press. I thought all that was working, it was just at that top end we weren't getting those chances. We had a meeting with the players, I think after the Aberdeen game, and all of a sudden we started to kick on. Ross County away was a big game as well, but they are all big games.

Tannadice, though, offered a positive glimpse to the near future, with Melamed claiming his first goal.

Guy Melamed

I felt like I had to prove to everyone, and myself, that I could score goals in Scotland and that I deserved to be in the first XI. I felt very satisfied after that game and I think my number of goals for St Johnstone was good for the minutes I played. I scored seven times (in 23 appearances) and I'm sure I would have got more than 10 in the league if everything had been normal when I first came to Perth.

The players were very happy for me after my goal against United. They knew how hard I had worked. I stayed behind after training just to be ready for my chance. The players and coaches at the club are all quality people. The atmosphere was very good. I was a foreigner but they made me feel I was in a good place.

When we didn't start the season well, everyone was still so positive and when I scored against Dundee United I really felt I was contributing to the team.

The Israeli and Kane started in attack together again against St Mirren and Saints achieved the perfect semi-final lift with a 1-0 win, thanks to Kane's strike shortly after half-time.

Steven MacLean
When Guy came in, you could see he was a good player, and it just took him time to get up to speed – and we gave him that time. He is a top, top finisher. He is probably one of the most gifted finishers I've worked with. His movement and his actual finishing are very, very good. He proved that when he played for us. He is technically very good.

Stevie May
I think it was good in terms of the three of us as forwards, all completely different in near enough every way in how we play. It allowed the manager to kind of pick and choose players depending on winning the game and depending on what formation our team were facing. We all played with each other at some point. Kano obviously probably played more games last season than he has in his whole time here, and he did brilliantly. I'm buzzing for him and I think everyone was delighted for him to do so well. Obviously, on the back of performances from him and the squad as a whole, we managed to achieve results, and it's just a kind of reward for the hard work that's gone in over the years from more or less everyone at the club.

Jason Kerr
I think Guy played a massive part in our season, and especially when he also played with Kano. I thought they complemented

each other really well, and he came up with a few good goals. The strikers definitely played a key part in the season.

Liam Gordon

Kano was a revelation. He was just amazing off the ball, he always gives you that, but on the ball, I just thought we saw a different player last season – he was superb. And Guy played a massive part, he scored some crucial goals.

Stevie May

Kano and Guy were playing and scoring, and after the 2-2 draw at United we went on to get results. I was coming off the bench and affecting games from there, and they were starting well, so you kind of stick with what's gone well at the time. It would have been unfair for them to have been dropping out of the team. It was kind of working and you don't want to change things too much.

The players certainly didn't know at the time, but they were already starting to put together the greatest run of results in St Johnstone's 137-year history. From the 0-0 draw with Hamilton at McDiarmid Park on 30 December to the end of the campaign, Saints contested 25 games and lost just four – two of them against Celtic.

Callum Davidson

It has to be the best period in the club's history, without a doubt. I think that was all down to the hard work we had done beforehand, that belief in how we were playing. It just started to click. I think everyone started performing to a level that was so high. They demanded it off each other and that became a norm for us. We were going into each match, even Rangers and Celtic games, thinking we had a chance of getting a result. That all, for me, culminates in the semi-final of the Betfred.

Hibs were huge favourites, especially as it was fourth versus eighth with 17 points separating Jack Ross's men and their Premiership opponents. Saints also had the weight of history to deal with. The Hampden Park clash was the club's 11th League Cup semi-final, but they had only made the final twice (1969 and 1998) and failed to win the competition. The statisticians weren't slow to also highlight that Saints' last win at Hampden was a 1-0 win over Queen's Park on lowly Division 2 duty in 1987. Perth fans were well used to fruitless trips to the national stadium – even if on this occasion they couldn't attend anyway as the pandemic continued to grip. Think of the 1992 League Cup last-four loss to Rangers at Hampden, likewise in 2010. Scottish Cup semi-final heartache at Hampden was also a familiar feeling. Yet Saints had consistently proved stubborn opponents for Hibs and there was a growing confidence within the McDiarmid Park squad.

Scott Tanser

We stuck to our usual build-up, no hotel stay or anything like that, and there were the Covid checks that we had got used to. Everyone had us down as massive underdogs going into the game but I'm not sure why. We had a great record against them. We knew we had a better team player for player and we backed ourselves to win. We had nothing to fear.

Davidson, with face mask on, enjoyed a pre-match coffee outside a café at Hampden. Little did he know the same image would be repeated on social media as the season continued.

Callum Davidson

Guy had scored against United, but I had it in my head that I was going to play a front three against Hibs. In big games, against really good opposition, I normally play a three because I believe it is the right system to play. With a two, teams can sometimes get at us too easily down the sides. People probably gave me a bit of stick for not playing Guy, so it was a big call to make but I believed it was the right team to pick. Fortunately, the decisions I made turned out to be good ones and hopefully that continues. It was how I felt we could hurt Hibs, at the same time sort of negating their attacking threat, which was fantastic.

David Wotherspoon
We went in as the underdogs, Hibs were massive favourites. But we knew if we performed to our best we could win the game.

Callum Davidson
It was really eerie. I remember 10 minutes into the game, it's obviously a long way between the dugout and the little box you stand in, and thinking it was really strange; I could hear Jack shout, me shout, the players shout, echoing. Then you get lost in the game. Supporters not being there for that five-month period, and some of the craziness that we did, like scoring near the end against Ross County to get us into the top six, the Rangers cup game at Ibrox, those are the things fans missed out on, and the players as well. You don't realise how much it means to the players. Yes, fans boo, criticise, but those are the times you live for as a player. It's that entertainment value that was lost as we played through a pandemic. In the first 20 minutes against Hibs, you would say we were nervous, not quite sure, a little bit edgy and then after that I just thought we played really well.

Zander Clark
It was a big first half hour. Going into it, we felt we had to start well but unfortunately for us, we were a slow burner. We were right under the cosh for the first 25 minutes or so. Fair play to Hibs, they started on the front foot and we couldn't get a foothold in the game. There was the chance from (Paul) Hanlon

that I made the save from. Then the ball came back in, I made the save from (Jamie) Murphy and then he managed to dink it and it hit the bar. (Jackson) Irvine had a couple of headers that just flashed by the post. You sort of think 'the next chance we get, we need to take it'. Thankfully, we did. The momentum of the whole game changed when we went 1-0 up. We got a lift.

James Brown

The semi-final was the first game I was on the bench. When I first spoke to the gaffer and the boys, they were just like, 'we're not playing badly, we just can't put the ball in the net and we can't score', and stuff like that. I know it's a cliché, everyone says it's a fine margin, but it is – goals change games at the end of the day. You see how a game's going and one goal goes in and the whole dimension changes.

Jason Kerr

We were kind of on the back foot, the whole 30 minutes before the goal. Hibs were obviously playing really well and they missed a few good chances. Zander made a good few saves, so we were up against it. And I think the 35th minute was maybe one of the two times we got up the pitch and we managed to get a corner which Spoony took. I've run up to the corner, and I was like, 'I'm knackered!' I feel like we are really effective in the box, in both boxes, so it was good when we managed to get a goal. I just felt like I ran forward and then managed to lose (Ryan) Porteous – he was kind of running back – and I felt I was always going to win the header.

And to score at that point, it was amazing, I don't think my pals were happy with me, they were fuming, but it was a really good moment for me. It took the pressure off a wee bit and we managed to get to half-time one up, and after that, we never looked back.

Alistair Stevenson

I thought it was a great honour for Jason to be named as captain back in 2019. I wondered if it would be too much for him to take on, but he seems to have thrived on it. We got him from Tynecastle Boys' club and he came straight into academy football at the top end. He was a midfielder, initially, but after a wee bit of coaxing he decided he was prepared to play at centre half. We could see that was a really good position for him. He has the ability, as a midfielder, to pass the ball from the back really well. He is composed, he can pass it and he is maybe one that does like to come out from the back. But he always gets back and, for me, he is just a real quality player now. He always had big potential, but he has the bit between his teeth now and has formed a great partnership with Liam and Jamie at the back. They seem to relish playing together.

David Wotherspoon

We had our scares in the first sort of 20 minutes, where they hit the bar and had chances. But we rode our luck and it felt like the 2014 Scottish Cup Final again. Dundee United hit the post that year at 0-0 and had chances. Against Hibs, we felt like it was going to be our day. We scored just before half-time which settled the nerves and got us into a confident mood.

Scott Tanser

I made 36 appearances and that was one of the best games I was involved in all season, along with the Rangers quarter-final in the Scottish Cup. As soon as we got that first goal we kicked on.

That was my first taste of playing at Hampden. It was very strange not having fans there. You hear absolutely everything. You want to go out onto the pitch beforehand and hear the fans in games like that. But, of course, it was eerily quiet. It had a stranger feeling than the league games because it was such a big occasion.

Craig Conway

We rode our luck early on with Hibs hitting the bar and Murphy missing a chance. I remember thinking then it might just be our day. We came into the game more and more. Once we got our noses in front we didn't look back.

After Kerr's headed opener shortly before the break, up popped Rooney with a powerful header from a Conway delivery on 49 minutes. Hibs were shell-shocked.

Shaun Rooney

We had worked on the set-pieces on the Friday. Obviously, it was the one I scored, that was worked on as well. With the opener, big 'Jase' always likes running to the back post, that's always his run, so you know if anybody runs there, then you'll get moaned at by him, and that's something you don't want – to get moaned at! 'Macca' did all that on the Friday, and it worked well on the day.

I have scored quite a few headed goals. My very first professional goal was with Queen's Park. I scored with my head with that one. I've always liked heading the ball, I always enjoy going and attacking the ball, and with my position, as well, trying to get into the back post.

The nickname of the 'Bellshill Cafu' continued to grow, as rampaging Rooney set up the third for Conway at the back post on 63 minutes. It was game over. Saints were final bound.

David Wotherspoon

To beat them 3-0 was just so convincing that it gave us massive belief going into the rest of the season.

Shaun Rooney

I think after it went 2-0, the game sort of opened up more, as well, so it gave me a bit more freedom to run up and down the pitch. That's what I like to do, so I just kept on running!

Danny McNamara

It was great to see Shaun doing so well. He and I drove each other on in the first half of the season. Shaun is a great guy, funny and a bit crazy. But he's one of the nicest lads I've met, such a humble guy. We were competing for the same position when I was there, but he was nothing but positive with me.

Obviously, Shaun was brilliant after I left and really pushed on. With the way Callum likes to play, he wants crosses in from wide areas and Shaun is such a threat coming in from the side. You saw that with his goals. If they hang it up to him there is only going to be one winner.

Callum Davidson

Shaun had obviously played a few games, in at centre-half, then in at wing-back. He was getting better and he works unbelievably hard in training, doing runs. He didn't sulk, he could easily have said 'why am I not playing?' He didn't do it once. He just worked hard, started to listen. When Danny was playing that well, I couldn't get Shaun in the team. He came in and hit the ground running as he was determined to do well. That's something I like about his character. He is a little bit daft at times, but he was brilliant.

Craig Conway

I felt we were comfortable in the second half and could even have gone on to score more. The defence developed in confidence as the season went on. That was a massive part of our success.

The central defenders are all relatively young. They grew in stature and that comes with experience. They set really high standards in every game towards the end of the campaign. That win over Hibs definitely gave us belief. The formation had clicked and it was a real squad effort, everyone was playing their part and the manager wasn't scared of rotating the attacking players.

Jason Kerr

I think that was the best we had ever played in the season, we were magnificent. We went on to score another two good goals, and there could have been more. We absolutely blew them away.

Scott Tanser

There was a lot of hype about Hibs' attacking threat and they relied massively on their front three. But our back five shut them out and we could go on and play our own game.

It was great to have the three centre-backs fit almost all season. That was a massive bonus for us. They were just so steady and the team was built around the foundation they provided. In other positions, players could come in and be trusted to do their jobs.

James Brown

Especially in the second half of the season, with our three centre-halves, we were solid. Then all you've got to do is nick one or two, because the majority of times we were keeping clean sheets.

Gordon, a boyhood Saints fan and former Perth High pupil like Wotherspoon, was among those thriving.

Alistair Stevenson

Liam is a local boy and I got the opportunity to get him back from Hearts. I think he is just a fantastic competitor, very brave, makes tackles, wins headers, puts his body on the line. He is not a match winner at the other end of the park in terms of scoring goals, but he is a match winner in defence as he blocks everything that is coming through. I think he has been absolutely fantastic.

He is so dedicated. He will always want to work on what he thinks his weaknesses are. He keeps himself fit and healthy. He gets a lot of knocks because he is so physical but I think he has come on leaps and bounds. He is definitely a great defender.

Callum Davidson

I think at that point the players thought 'wow'. I think that was the game that gave the players the belief that they were a good team and can win games of football, no matter what system they play. They had just won a semi-final 3-0 against Hibs and that was it for me. That for me was the game that turned our season.

25 January 2021 Newsflash . . .
  'Glenn Middleton: St Johnstone sign Rangers winger on loan for the remainder of the season' (BBC online)

Glenn Middleton, Forward, 21

I felt a lot of respect from the manager when he first spoke to me about a loan. As soon as I turned up for the first day in training I realised pretty quickly I had made the right decision.

There was a real togetherness about everyone. I know players often say that about teams but it stood out straight away for me. You don't get that everywhere. The goals and results hadn't been coming earlier but the boys had been working hard and that turned in the second half of the season.

I knew when I signed I couldn't play in the Betfred Cup. I had played as a sub for Rangers at Falkirk earlier in the season. I would be lying if I said it wasn't frustrating sitting it out. But I had to continue to do the right things on a daily basis. That is the only way you're going to move forward.

I had to be ready for my chance and watching the lads go on to win the cup gave me even more drive to be involved in occasions like that in the future. But I didn't think it would be a few months later with St Johnstone! You couldn't write that script.

A draw with Aberdeen maintained momentum, before the Perth men closed out the month in stunning comeback style at Kilmarnock to ease away from relegation trouble. From 2-0 down at half-time, Melamed, Davidson and McCann all struck in a thrilling 19-minute spell.

Steven MacLean

The one game I remember speaking to Callum at the side was losing 2-0 to Kilmarnock away. He came across and said, 'What do you think?' I said, 'We've been excellent. We've lost two goals from bad decision-making and probably bad defending, but apart from that you wouldn't change anything. We've been brilliant.' He said, 'I know.' We went in at half-time, and rather than being tempted to change things, we stuck with it, and the boys went out and scored three goals in the second half. You say to yourself, 'it's just football' at times. Sometimes you do everything right, but you don't get what you deserve. I think that day could have been a turning point as well. It was a big part of the season. I think they were above us that day and we dragged them back towards us with the 3-2 win. They ended up relegated and we went on to finish fifth.

Callum Davidson

I was kicking things at half-time. We dominated, had chance after chance after chance. Killie basically broke and scored two goals. I said at half-time, 'Just believe in what we're doing, don't panic, keeping doing certain things and you'll get chances.' It was a brilliant comeback, an absolutely fantastic comeback.

Ali McCann

It was a big second half at Killie. It was a strange one because I felt we actually played quite well in the first half and found ourselves 2-0 down. I thought 'we probably don't deserve this given the way we passed the ball'. We just felt if we got the next goal we had every chance, but to go from 2-0 down to a 3-2 win, it was brilliant. It kick-started a good run of form.

Alistair Stevenson

Ali was a late developer. He played with the youth academy and came from a fair distance down the east coast, but he made the effort to get there all the time. A lot of people said he maybe needed to be a wee bit quicker, but I could see he was quick up top and had a fantastic football brain. Due to the attitude he has, he has trained harder, and harder, and harder. He never misses training and he has deservedly got where he is today because of the effort he has put in, his attitude and his ability.

Saints were clicking into gear. Engines were revved for a Betfred League Cup Final date with Livingston looming large on the road ahead.

FIVE

HISTORY BOYS

'Scottish football is a better place when honours are shared;
St Johnstone have now ended Celtic's run of consecutive
trophies at the 12 mark.'
Ewan Murray, The Guardian

28 February 2021, Hampden Park
Betfred League Cup Final: Livingston 0, St Johnstone 1
*Clark; Rooney, Kerr, Gordon, McCart, Booth; Craig, McCann;
Conway (May), Kane, Wotherspoon.*
Goal: Rooney 32.

*February is a short month, yet it seemed to take an eternity for
Saints fans still in the grip of Covid-19 lockdown. The club, to
their credit, engaged with supporters wonderfully in the final
build-up with all manner of social media activities, together
with a commemorative souvenir magazine. After all, Saints were
aiming for third time lucky in the League Cup after coming close
in 1969, a 1-0 defeat to Jock Stein's Celtic, and a 2-1 loss to
Rangers in 1998. Finals don't come around too often for all those
of a Perth persuasion, or so we thought.*

In the lead-up, narrow defeats to the Old Firm were sandwiched by a hugely significant 2-1 league win at Livingston – with that man Rooney scoring once more. Livi had been on a roll, their early-season form earning plaudits and a European bid under reformed manager, David Martindale. Saints, however, appeared to be starting to peak at just the right time. They were now firmly in the hunt for a top-six finish themselves, just two points off the top half and only nine behind Livi in fifth.

James Brown

I started at Rangers when we lost 1-0, it was nice to go straight in. To be fair, we sort of started to turn the corner as a squad. We won at Livi and it was nice to come into it when all the boys were starting to pick up results. Obviously, Shaun was playing bang on form. So often, if there's someone like that, you've just got to sit back and there's not a lot you can do. I didn't play for a while, as he was flying.

Liam Craig

Livi away, winning there, it killed their run and probably gave us that psychological belief that we could beat them.

Craig Bryson

We really started to gel and I think the experience helped. I think sometimes at clubs the experienced players play a different role from Monday-Friday that a lot of the fans don't see. The older lads keep up the morale when things aren't going well and they have a good bit of banter with the younger lads. But when it comes to seeing someone not putting in the work or not doing their job properly, then you are there to use your experience and help them. I think you need a good balance of older and younger players. Jason is a young captain, he has flourished, had an incredible season, but Liam (Craig) was there all the way to help him.

Then I think it helps Ali (McCann) having players like myself, Liam and Murray next to him. I've had to adapt my game a lot at St Johnstone. I used to be a little like Ali when I was younger. Now I've adapted my game, I play the more experienced role and let him do his thing and flourish. The gaffer has built a really good squad here and there is a great team spirit.

Davidson's men would give themselves the perfect cup final boost with a convincing 3-0 away win at Motherwell, a first-class team display, with Melamed netting twice. Yet, the tone for such a performance had again been set on the training field.

Liam Craig

Going back 10 days before the League Cup Final, to the Wednesday, the manager sent us in from training. The manager has standards and we weren't meeting them. He sets the expectations. Ten days before a cup final, three days before a massive game at Motherwell, and he sent us in from training. That was probably a good thing for the players because it just stopped us getting ahead of ourselves. Thursday was a day off and it made us come back in on the Friday and training was excellent. We went to Motherwell and I'll never forget the manager telling us 'we have got four games before the split'. No talk about the cup final. 'If we get 10 points we give ourselves every opportunity.' We went out that day and won 3-0 and it could have been five or six. It set the tone for the cup final week.

Callum Davidson

That was a great performance at Motherwell. The performance levels that day were right up there, with everything going right. The lads were so focused. The effort we put in to reach the top six is probably something not really written about.

Guy Melamed

People always ask me if I am right or left-footed. In the 3-0 win over Motherwell I scored a goal from 25 yards with my left foot but took the penalty with my right. Once when I was injured, I couldn't kick with my right foot so I trained and used my left. That helped me a lot.

Yet, for all the Perth positivity, there was agony once more for midfielder Davidson. Injured for the 2014 Scottish Cup Final, his testimonial year put on hold due to Covid and then Hampden heartache.

Murray Davidson, Midfielder, 33

It was difficult to take, missing the Betfred Cup Final, after we had done so well in seeing off Hibs in the semi. There was a big difference for me between the 2021 finals and 2014. I hadn't really played a part seven years earlier because of injury. This time I had been contributing. But I felt my calf going against Rangers at Ibrox in February. It was just the second muscle injury I have ever had in my career. I didn't know the extent of it until we got the scan results back. It was touch and go but the rehab went well. I was sure I would make it. We had to push it. But then I felt it go again late on in the last of the rehab sessions we had planned.

The next few days were hard when it sank in that I wouldn't make the final against Livingston. My phone was off most of the time and family left me alone to get my head right. But I had to get myself right to be the best team-mate I could be. I was more gutted for my parents – Liz and Ronnie – family and friends at missing the Betfred Final. It was tough though. I don't mind admitting it.

The names of Mackay, Anderson, Millar, Wright, MacLean and co hold heroic status at McDiarmid Park, given their feats in 2014. It was now time for a new team to be etched into St Johnstone folklore.

Zander Clark

We were fully aware it was a chance to go and make ourselves sort of legends in terms of winning the League Cup for the first time for the club. You look at the boys from 2014 and they will always be legends. We thought this was our chance to go and grab a bit of that as well.

Liam Craig

You remember conversations during the season. Like speaking to the manager and Macca before the League Cup Final and the manager saying he had never won a cup as a player.

For Craig, it was a hugely emotional time. He had missed Scottish Cup successes with both Hibs and St Johnstone. At the age of 34, he was desperate for silverware. He was desperate to start. His own personal story and his love and affection for the club were obvious as Saints prepared to head for Hampden.

Liam Craig

I just felt the Livi game was my opportunity to go and be a part of a cup final, something I'd never done, never mind the two cup finals I had missed! At that point, I'd lost seven semi-finals, I think, throughout my career, and watching St Johnstone win in 2014, I can still remember sitting in my living room with Calvin, Jessica and (wife) Laura, buzzing for the players, because I'd done so much with the majority of that squad – and got to know their families.

The bit that hit me the most was seeing them on the park with their families after the game – that's what hit me harder than them winning the cup, because that's what I wanted with my family.

Instead, I got to miss out on it in two cup finals last season!
But, looking back to 2014, that's what I wanted. David Gray at
Hibs is one of my best mates, and the one thing that annoyed
me when Hibs won the Scottish Cup in 2016 (for the first time
since 1902) was that he didn't get that moment with his family
on the park, because of everything that happened post-match.
Hibs winning the cup didn't hurt me at all. I was delighted for
them, because I know how hard that group of players, just like
at St Johnstone, had worked. I was buzzing for Paul Hanlon and
Lewis Stevenson, because I knew what they'd been through at
Hibs to get to that moment and how much it would mean to
them. And you would never, ever want someone that you were
so close to not to go and achieve something like that.

I just felt with the Livingston game it was my chance. It's
stupid, because people say, 'ah, it's just another game'. It's not
just another game. I had played at Livi when we beat them 2-1
three weeks before the cup final, and I came home that night
and I said to Laura, 'The way we played, there's a good chance
now that I'll maybe play in the cup final.' It was probably in my
psyche as that's probably the only time we've beaten them when
I've played and it gave me a good chance.

Coming in on the Monday morning before the final, Laura
had sent me a card from the kids to the stadium, and it's at
my place, and you open it and it's pictures of me and the kids
sharing moments on the park down the years, and the memories
we've got. I'd never won a cup final, the kids weren't born when
I won the First Division, so when we finished third to qualify
for Europe (in 2013), I brought Calvin onto the pitch with me,
doing a lap. I love all that.

So seeing all that on Monday, you know I wouldn't go as far as
to say it brings a tear to your eye, but certainly it hits you – this
is what it's all about. It's not like any other game.

In terms of how much sacrifice and dedication you put into

football, with so many people helping me to get to that stage, I knew it was a big game. I also knew at 34 years old, it was now or never. And then I drove through Perth on the Saturday after training because I wanted to take everything in. I saw the banner at the Broxden Roundabout, I saw the social media. Due to Covid, you couldn't really get about personally to see the fans. So I did that drive through the city, through the centre, just thinking and looking at everything and seeing how much it would mean to so many people if we could go and win it.

Then I went home that afternoon from training, walked in and the kids were buzzing, there were balloons everywhere, balloons with St Johnstone badges on them, flags up. So, again, the kids… it was just massively everyone buying into it. And people say it's like any other week. Well, see if you get there every season, it might be like any other game. See when it's the first time in your career and you've been playing full-time since you were 16 and you're 34 – it's not like any other week.

The morning of the game, I was waiting for the team bus, standing at the bus stop and Alex Ferguson was there too. I was speaking to 'Fergie' and just telling him, 'Go and enjoy it whatever, if you're on the bench, if you're in the squad. You're in the squad, a cup final squad, at 17 years old.' I said, 'I'm 34 and it's the first time I've been in a cup final squad.' I said, 'Take it all in.'

The Perth boss made just one change as Conway came into the side at the expense of Melamed. Martindale brought Steve Lawson, Marvin Bartley and Scott Robinson into his team, Bartley a surprise choice at left midfield to try and counteract Rooney. Craig still had time to think about his fellow long-serving midfield colleague, Davidson.

Liam Craig

Murray's performance in the semi-final was sensational against

Hibs. It epitomised everything that Murray's about, and what the club's about. For him to miss out on the League Cup Final, I was genuinely devastated for him, because, again, people know what I've been through in my career in terms of missing out on cup finals. He was at the club and missed out on that 2014 cup final, and then he missed out on another one.

We had our changing room bubbles, and he was in mine, and speaking to him on the Friday, just me and him in the dressing room, that was huge. It just showed, again, how big a character and how big a team-mate he is – and that's what epitomises the whole squad. But the good thing about St Johnstone is – and it's always been like this since I first came to the club – that togetherness, that spirit. There haven't been any big time Charlies, and if there have been, they're out the door quicker than they came in the door. That togetherness and that group: Fran (Sandaza) coming in for one year, he buys into it. Jody Morris came from Chelsea and Leeds, Michael Duberry, with his Leeds background too, bought into St Johnstone, bought into Perth, bought into the fan base. Yes, it's not the biggest but – Tommy has said it in the past as well – that spirit that we've got, you can't buy that. And people wanting their team-mates and the team to do well last season showed that more than any other.

The talking was almost over. In surreal, behind-closed door circumstances, Saints sought the League Cup for the first time since their formation in 1884.

Liam Craig
I remember walking on the park before it, there was just a buzz about it. Maybe I'm just a traditionalist, but it meant so much being at Hampden for the cup final – even though there was nobody there.

Looking at it, with Marvin (Bartley) starting at left midfield it was incredible, because that week, when the manager said I was starting, I felt, 'if I'm better than Marvin in the middle of the park, we win the game'. That was my mind-set, because I felt what Marvin's great at with Livi is that he breaks it up, keeps the ball moving, he lets (Jason) Holt and he lets (Scott) Pittman run on and support the striker, which gives me a problem.

17 mins *'Robinson, does really well to hold it up for... Mullin! Oh, he is so close to the opening goal but for a wonder save from Zander Clark at full stretch.' (Premier Sports)*

Zander Clark

I made a save early on from (Josh) Mullin. He caught it sweetly and I just managed to get fingertips to it and push it round the post. It was a cagey affair. It was probably going to be one goal to win the game.

David Wotherspoon

We know what type of team Livingston is, it is always a battle against them no matter what. They fight for everything and we knew we had to do the dirty side of the game as much as we could to win our battles. We fought really hard in the middle of the park, the back three were tremendous again and the wing-backs were up and down all day, stopping their counter attacks. The strikers worked so hard too, such a thankless task up front sometimes, for the team.

Liam Craig

When Marvin went to left midfield I thought initially, 'he knows we're going to put it on top, maybe it's just kick-off, maybe he's just starting there, and he'll come into the middle of the park'. And as the game went on, it was me and Ali against their three, and although we were outnumbered, it was Lawson, Pittman and Holt, three good footballers, but they don't have that physicality – none of those are going to be physically stronger than me in the middle of the park. So, if the game got scrappy, I was comfortable that Ali and I were going to dominate. And it wasn't until 70 minutes that Marvin came back in.

Zander made a great save off Mullin, and that was their only real chance. Everything else I thought we were comfortable with, without really imposing ourselves on the game.

32 mins 'There's Rooney. Oh, he's done it again. Shaun Rooney. And is that the first step to glory for St Johnstone.' (Premier Sports)

Craig Conway

Getting even one cup winner's medal wasn't on the agenda when I signed. But that all changed after beating Hibs. It's fair enough getting to a final but when you get that far you have to put everything into winning it.

David Wotherspoon

Craig (Conway) put in the corner for Shaun to score the winning header. His deliveries were excellent. The semi-final against Hibs, as well, he was running all day and was always available. Again, he provided a set piece . . . and a goal. We got another set piece against Livi and it was a massive goal at a massive stage. Shaun loved it.

Shaun Rooney

It was a move we had worked on, again. We work on the set pieces and it was another Conway cross. Obviously, I scored three weeks before the cup final against them with a header, so I always felt, myself, I could score a header.

Zander Clark

Shaun is mental, honestly! But he's brilliant to have about the place. There is a never a dull day in the changing room when he is about. He is always wanting to sing or just be as loud as he can to try and bring the mood of the place up. With his performances on the park, it's not as if he has a carry on when he gets over that white line – he means business. He has been excellent for us.

Callum Davidson

It was a really tough game. I gave Livi a lot of credit for their run, especially mid-season. They are a really tough, physical team to play against. They knew how to win games of football. We had obviously beaten them just previously in the league. It was one of those games we knew we had to fight and scrap. We knew we could do that, we knew we could compete against their physical side. Again, Shaun pops up with a magnificent header. And again it's Craig who has delivered it, as he did in the semi-final. He probably doesn't get that credit, as everyone just looks at the goalscorer. It's a fantastic header, just pure aggression. For someone to score in the quarter-final, semi-final and final as a right wing-back is quite an incredible story.

45+2 mins 'McCann to Rooney, he's going to try one from range . . . and why not, he caught it well.' (Premier Sports)

Liam Craig

I was probably a bit harsh after the game, saying that it wasn't a great game. We probably managed the game quite well, rather than playing well. But the first time we really got in, Shaun got in behind and won the corner. It was a great delivery from Craig, and Shaun scored. And I always remember never celebrating that much at the goal. I didn't even run up the park, because my focus was, 'right, we're not getting beaten', and that was it. I'll celebrate after the game.

46 mins *'It's Ali McCann across, oh it's a great save by Robby McCrorie (from Wotherspoon)!' (Premier Sports)*

Liam Craig
I thought for 20 minutes we were excellent, at the start of the second half, dominating the game, playing on the front foot. We just needed to get another goal.

56 mins *'Kane with the flick-on to get Wotherspoon in, McCrorie thought about it . . . Wotherspoon goes down. He asked the question, no penalty for St Johnstone'. (Premier Sports)*

Liam Craig
They staved off a second goal. If we went 2-0 up, the game would have been done.

David Wotherspoon
We just hung on from there, we knew we could defend well and we just ground it out. We had players who could come on and give us fresh legs (May for Conway) and still do the same job. It was credit to everyone on the day to get over the line.

Callum Davidson
From the goal, I didn't think we were really under much threat. People say 'why did you not make more changes?' I was actually pretty comfortable. My family were pacing around rooms, jumping over sofas and stuff but I was pretty comfortable. I didn't really want to make that many changes as the boys were playing so well.

In the closing stages, Saints were under an aerial bombardment. But time and time again, Davidson's organised outfit stayed resolute, heading and clearing away.

90+2 mins *'And St Johnstone drop to their knees in celebration! Callum Davidson and St Johnstone seize their moment! It is their day to shine in the Hampden sun.' (Premier Sports)*

Liam Craig

I'll never forget the last minute: the ball goes up… I go to head it, it goes back, goes up again, 'Jammo' wins a header, 'Boothy' winning headers, and that's the game it sort of turned into. The back three were incredible over that period, along with Zander, and then Rooney's breaking, and I'm just shouting at Don (Robertson), the ref, just going, 'blow the whistle!' with a swear word in there as well! Then when he blew the whistle, I genuinely just fell to my knees, right there, and the tears came right away. I said I'd always be happy with my career, but to win something, and to win that way with St Johnstone, was even better. And to win at Hampden was just incredible.

For the Perth Saints, their wait for League Cup glory was over. Just like against Dundee United in 2014, they had seized their final opportunity. Saints, remarkably, also became just the fifth team in Scotland to win more than one trophy in the 21st century.

Craig Conway

It was pretty comfortable overall. We knew what to expect from Livingston and we were really strong. It was an amazing feeling to win a cup with St Johnstone and by that time belief in the squad was sky high. We felt we could take on anyone.

Steven MacLean

It was huge to win the League Cup. People talk about the Scottish Cup, the one that probably everyone wants to win, but the League Cup is just as big for me. The achievement in itself was superb. It sort of finished it off for the club as well, now they have won the Scottish Cup and the League Cup. It is great to say they have done both.

Callum Davidson
I was buzzing, delighted, absolutely thrilled to do it. It's a massive trophy. It's a cup St Johnstone had never won. To win it in my first year, very similar to Tommy with the Scottish Cup, it was like 'wow, that was brilliant, amazing'. It was such a great feeling for the players.

Murray Davidson
There was no use me moping around feeling sorry for myself. I tried to support the boys as best I could. I was as happy as anyone when we won the Betfred Final.

Again, for Craig, there was extra emotion in the immediate celebrations – there had to be.

Liam Craig
I would've always been pleased with what I've done and the amount of games I've played in my career. But now you look back and you think 'I've got something to show for it'. I had to gather myself, because you want to go and enjoy it, try and take it all in, but it was difficult. Macca came on, and he's seen the tears; I remember him saying to me, 'You need to stop it; you'll set me off here!' Macca's been part of my career the last seven or eight years so he knew how I felt. The young boys celebrated it and got the buzz of it and hopefully will go and win more, but for me at 34, and after what I'd done in my career, those losing semi-finals, didn't play against Hibs in the semi-final in the League Cup, to have my day in the sun, on the 28th of February, it was just incredible. And getting your hands on that trophy – you can see what it meant to me.

Later, in an iconic picture, Craig was captured on his haunches, alone on the pitch at a deserted Hampden, FaceTiming his family. The photo will be framed sometime . . .

Liam Craig

I'd gone into the changing room and the players were celebrating, and honestly, the tears came then, just because I'd turned my phone on and all the messages were coming through! People that you don't speak to every day, but have been a big part of your career, like ex-coaches, managers, players, family members, everything, supporters on social media, and it just hits you. And I thought, 'I need to get out of here. I need to go and speak to Laura; I need to go and speak to the kids.' As I said, the one thing I always wanted was to celebrate with them after a cup final, on the pitch, and I suppose that was my way of doing it, in terms of going out and FaceTiming them, and I kept saying to them on the phone, 'I don't know why I'm crying'. Because the emotion does just come over you. Maybe seeing the kids and that, as well, it was incredible.

And obviously Matty (Gallagher, *Perthshire Advertiser*) takes that picture . . . and you're sort of gathering your thoughts, you're speaking to the family. Like, Laura's been through more than anything with me, she's had to put up with so much in terms of all the downsides, and it's mad, because when I go home on a Saturday night when we've been beaten, I'm just sitting in the house not knowing what to do, and when you win, I'm out with Zander or you're out with one of the boys! So she's been through it all and been a huge part of it, even when I left Hibs and I couldn't get a club. Speaking to her, she was honest, in terms of when I came back to St Johnstone. I had opportunities to go elsewhere, but she didn't want me to do it, and we had, obviously, good conversations about that. She's probably one of the reasons that I didn't sign with someone else before coming back to St Johnstone, like Guiseley and the part-time stuff down the road, because she just didn't want me to do it.

So, it was massive for me, speaking to them after the final. The picture isn't framed yet, it's still just on my phone. It's still a picture that I'll always look at. And the good thing that other people haven't seen is that I've got the picture as a screen shot of me speaking to all of them on the park. So that's what I see, but me on the park is what everyone else sees. I quite like just the contrast between the two pictures.

Callum Davidson

Liam finished the season with very close to the most club appearances, over 400, just behind 'Ando' (Steven Anderson). He went away to Hibs and got a lot of stick for missing our 2014 Scottish Cup win. He was out of the team. I remember he came to see me and asked 'what is my role here?' I said 'your role is to play when you need to and perform well'. Murray got injured, unfortunately for Murray. I always say to players they have to be ready and one thing Liam Craig is, is ready. Once Murray got injured, Liam was absolutely fantastic in that spell. He has sort of changed his position. For me, to see him win that trophy, to be a huge part of it, was a massive delight. I was really pleased Liam was able to achieve that in his career.

As Davidson said, fans were pacing around living rooms for the final whistle before hugging their nearest and dearest in pure jubilation. It was a disappointment not to be there, not to celebrate with friends and family like in 2014 at Celtic Park, but tens of thousands of supporters were not required for an historic moment to be a celebrated sporting fact.

David Wotherspoon

The Livingston final was probably the moment I realised it was a shame there were no fans there. When the full-time whistle goes, usually there is loads of noise. Then you go and pick up your medal and you go to lift the trophy. There is the eruption from us but there is not that same feeling of the crowd getting right behind it and continuing the celebrations for ages and ages. We went into the dressing room and because of the Covid situation you still couldn't really celebrate as much as you would. It was still a massive and special occasion I'll never forget. It was certainly the start of something special. We knew after that we didn't want to sit down and rest on it. We wanted to carry on and make it the best season we could.

Zander Clark

You sort of became accustomed to it, with no fans. It was actually becoming weird watching old games on the TV and seeing fans in the stands. In terms of the magnitude of the game, winning the League Cup for the first time in the club's history, not having friends, family and supporters in, it was probably the first time where you really did miss them. What a day it would have been for everybody.

Shaun Rooney

I had the 'pint machine' on when I went home. My dad, obviously, said, 'I'm coming up to your house to have a couple of pints with you.' I said, 'No problem,' so he came round and had a couple of beers with me. Brilliant.

Liam Craig

We won the game and there were six people on my bus back, so we're not even celebrating together. I think it was me, Mayso, Muzz, El and Liam Gordon, maybe Paul Mathers. Separate buses. So, people don't realise that: you can't celebrate together. So back on the bus, we had a few beers and a bottle of champagne, I think, and I phoned Laura. I said, 'please could you come and pick me up at six o'clock, at Stirling,' where I got dropped. I was just leaving my car there, because obviously I'd had a few beers. So, she came to pick me up with the kids, and I was back in the house for half-six. Drey Wright's father-in-law, believe it or not, had his own champagne business, and it's nice champagne. I'd been looking after Drey's dog, so he gave me a nice bottle. When he was going down to London, we'd always take the dog, because he just lived along the road from me. And I said, 'You know what? Now is a great time to open this'. I sat and had that with Laura, and had a great picture, again. Oliver is in his Toy Story jammies with the medal over his head, getting a picture taken, and all that, really enjoying it.

People say, 'ah, you missed the party,' but then I thought, 'you know what? I've actually come home relatively sober and enjoyed it with my family, and will remember it more'. It was just an unbelievable day and, to be honest, at that time, I thought, 'I can look back on my career now I've won something.' Obviously, I know I'd won the First Division, and at the time, Derek McInnes would say 'we can win a cup'. He did always say that, 'We can win a cup. We'll not win the Premier League, but we can win a cup.' But for me, I thought maybe winning the First Division was going to be as big as it got in terms of winning with St Johnstone.

Craig Bryson

After winning the Betfred Cup, we basically got sent home as we couldn't do anything as a team in the pandemic. We also had Hamilton to come in midweek, whoever arranged that! A couple of lads trained the day after the Betfred Cup Final who weren't in great nick to be honest – myself included. It's probably one of the worst training sessions of my life! But the older you get the more you appreciate just winning a trophy. The Hamilton game turned out to be a big game for us, in terms of fighting for the top six.

Callum Davidson

Unfortunately, again, there were no supporters. The biggest thing I remember from 2014 is going round the corner of the High Street on the open top bus and just seeing a sea of people. It's probably one of the highlights of my career doing that. It's just a shame we couldn't have done that with the players and the fans after the Betfred. It's probably one of the biggest regrets, when I think about it. I went back to the house and had a glass of champagne with my wife. There was nothing at the club that night for us all. It was a Sunday night and we had a huge game against Hamilton on the Wednesday night to try and get into the top six. I really enjoyed the Sunday night, I told the players to enjoy winning it, but we had huge games to come.

Liam Craig

Ali (McCann) had hurt his ribs in a challenge in the cup final so he missed the Hamilton game. We were 1-0 down at half-time, and we were coming back in and Ali walks onto the park, walks over to me and he's talking to me about the game, he's talking to me like what we can do better, where we can be better. That's when I thought, after the game, 'this is a player that isn't just going on the park and playing. He's thinking more about the game. He's actually becoming a leader at 21 years old'. For him to come to me and Bryso, Bryso's a month older than me, 34 as well, saying how he thinks we can go and get back in the game and win it, just shows that leadership quality. And he'll have learnt that working with Steve Davis and the Northern Ireland players as well.

It's been brilliant for me to see Ali develop over the last few years, and what he's done in the last two years is just incredible.

No one could have thought he was going to hit the heights to the extent he has in those two years. But the way he trains, the way he carries himself, is remarkable.

Ali McCann

Whoever I've played alongside, Liam, Muzz, Bryso or Spoony, they have all played hundreds of games at a high level and made my job so much easier. They talk you through it, do their bit that they have done for years and made my work easier. It helped me develop, being younger, and I enjoyed playing with them.

It's been brilliant to be involved with Northern Ireland. It's been quite surreal turning up and seeing all the people to play alongside. Steven Davis has been one, but there are plenty of senior players who have had good careers and carry themselves so well day-to-day. If I can take anything from them, it improves my game massively. Even the standard of the training, the intensity, has helped me a lot.

I watched the Euros final, Italy against England, in June. It was interesting to see Marco Verratti running rings around everyone else, not just me (after playing against him in a World Cup qualifier for Northern Ireland at the end of March)!

It was a great experience for me against Italy. It didn't quite sink in until the week was over, then looking back it was mad, to be fair. The way they played the game was so casual, but still so sharp and it was nothing I had experienced before. They are a really good team. I was pretty annoyed after the game that I didn't have the best performance, but then watching the game back it wasn't so bad after all. They were a different level, though, and I've now played against the European champions.

At Hamilton, step forward Melamed in the 87th minute for one of the goals of the season. Collecting a ball from Gordon in his path, he produced a Dennis Bergkamp-style finish to earn Saints a precious point.

Guy Melamed

My favourite goal is the one I scored at Hamilton. It was late in the game and we were losing 1-0. That draw kept us alive to qualify for the top six. I remember Liam Gordon getting the ball and I made a move against the defender because I know he can pass it long. Liam always plays with his head up to look for the movement of the strikers. He made a brilliant assist and I made a great touch. It was something I had worked on with Macca in training so I knew I could control it. That made it even better, doing it in a game.

Callum Davidson

To win the Betfred Cup and then do what we did on the Wednesday and Saturday was incredible. Basically, there were about six lads who couldn't train on the Monday (a little worse for wear). It was a massive effort against Hamilton, I actually thought we played really well. I made changes that I believed would win the game. It was one of those games, going back to earlier in the season, where we dominated most of the game, but Ross Callachan scored a cracker in the top corner. I'm thinking 'oh no'. But we kept pushing, kept believing. Guy produced a moment of magic. It was a great ball from Liam (Gordon), which he has got in his locker. For me, that is probably goal of the season, the way he took his touch and hit it quickly. That's what Guy has. In the following Hibs game, six days after the emotional high of Sunday, we came back and Liam (Craig) scored an absolute cracker. We just hung on, we fought and it showed the spirit, desire and hunger. I thought in the second half we probably looked a little bit dead on our feet. That was no fault of anybody, just the week we had. To come out with the three points against Hibs was enormous.

Liam Gordon

Guy had some crucial goals in that January, February run-in for the league. Some big goals, great performances. The one that stands out is his goal at Hamilton – that was brilliant.

Jason Kerr

What a touch that was.

Liam Gordon

I thought the pass was better! Seriously, another thing the manager's instilled in us is trying to give us that belief that we can all play, and the passing's great. But sometimes they're not long balls, they're long passes and into areas.

Jason Kerr

When we won the Betfred Cup, I knew we had a really good bunch of boys and we could go on and do something really special.

It wasn't long before that came to fruition.

SIX

ICONIC AT IBROX

'It's in from Craig. It's Zander Clark. It's in!
It's unbelievable. Zander Clark. Well, sometimes
football just comes up with the most unlikely of stories.'
Rory Hamilton, Commentator

Iconic: adjective; meaning very famous or popular.

In the up-and-down history of St Johnstone Football Club, the evening of Sunday 25 April 2021 on the south side of Glasgow certainly holds iconic status. It was a Scottish Cup quarter-final tie like no other.

Zander Clark
It was bonkers, that is the best way to describe it!

It is a match that will always raise a wide smile, such was the pure madness of it all. It also represented just how far this Saints side had come. In the weeks immediately preceding the daunting trip to Rangers – Steven Gerrard's dominant team had only lost in the Betfred League Cup to St Mirren all season – the Perth men had continued their feelgood factor.

Going back to 20 March, Davidson had challenged his side to claim a European spot after they snatched a Scottish Premiership top-six place in dramatic style with a late home winner against Ross County. It was a phenomenal effort, given Saints had not been in the top half of the division since September. Middleton's goal, coupled with Kyle Munro's 89th-minute equaliser for Hamilton against St Mirren, meant the Saints finished in the top six for the second year in a row – edging out the Buddies on goal difference by just two goals.

Glenn Middleton

That strike came from me still working hard in training. The manager trusted me enough to put me on when we were chasing the goal we needed to make the top six. When you get your chance you have to take it – thankfully I did just that. We knew we had to win that game but there was no sense of panic. There was a real trust in one another.

It was a massive sense of relief for me when I got that goal. I could feel a weight coming off my shoulders almost instantly. It was when we got back into the changing room that it began to sink in that we had made the top six. It was a good feeling, everyone was buzzing. It gave everyone the realisation that we were a very good team and that we could challenge anyone.

The results didn't all go our way after the split, but we knew we were there on merit. We took that belief into the Scottish Cup games and never looked back.

Guy Melamed

I think every goal I scored was important when I saw that we qualified for the top six on goal difference.

Callum Davidson

I remember with five minutes to go it was 0-0 and St Mirren were 1-0 up. We just couldn't score against County, then Liam threaded a great play to Mayso, he cut it back and Glenn swivelled and hit it into the corner. I was buzzing. Literally, two minutes later Paul Mathers shouts, 'It's 1-1! It's 1-1! (at Hamilton)' The games against Motherwell, Hamilton and Hibs were incredible games from the effort the players put in. It wasn't just 11 players, it was 20 players. Only 11 can play in games, but it was 20 players getting us there. It was an enormous effort to get us into the top six and something probably not really talked about, how well we did from where we were in October to get there.

A narrow league defeat at home to Aberdeen was sandwiched with Scottish Cup ties, firstly at Dens Park and then at home to Clyde. The very fact the competition was being played was pleasing for all, given fears the tournament would not be completed due to Covid-19. The suspension of all divisions below the Championship had caused the cup to be halted, but it restarted in late March with the final pushed back to allow it to finish. With games coming thick and fast, Saints maintained their momentum.

Guy Melamed

I also scored in the cup against Dundee and Clyde. Liam Gordon lives in Perth and he told me how important the Dundee cup game was for St Johnstone fans. I would love to have celebrated that one with our fans. Hopefully they come back to the stadiums in big numbers to support the guys. They are an incredible team with an incredible gaffer.

Jason Kerr

Liam (Gordon) did it again against Dundee, playing a similar kind of pass to Mayso that he had to find Guy in the league game at Hamilton. At Dens, Mayso set up Guy for the winner.

Liam Gordon

You've got strikers up there, the ones with the movement. They're all clever players and it makes our life easier, as well. If the ball's not onto the full-back or midfielder, if you've got strikers that are willing to peel in behind and give good movement, it's a joy for us to play to them.

Liam Craig

We had 10 days or so off coming into Dens and it wasn't the best performance.

Callum Davidson

It was one of those games against Dundee when we probably didn't play as well. The pitch was really sticky, difficult, and we were playing against local rivals. But, again, those are the type of games you need to win. We won on penalties against Dunfermline, we got through; the Motherwell tie we got through, and that was another game we got through. I felt pretty comfortable. I thought Dundee had a wee spell in the game, but we managed to see the game out professionally. All you want to be is in the next round.

Clark's late penalty-save from Charlie Adam ensured a safe passage at Dens – after the veteran midfielder had insisted the match wasn't a derby – before Melamed and O'Halloran sealed a routine win over Clyde. Suddenly, Davidson's side were in the last eight. Two games in four huge days against Rangers followed.

Callum Davidson

The pleasing thing about the game at Ibrox was having deservedly drawn against Rangers on the Wednesday in Perth, we set the tone a little bit for the game. I thought we played really well and Liam scored the penalty in the last minute. At that point, I think we deserved more than a draw. Rangers could thump you, they have the quality to do it, but we worked extremely hard as a unit.

Liam Craig

I really enjoy being able to sit now and let other players get forward and score goals, but it's always nice to pop up with a goal now and again, and I scored three big one's last season – one at Dundee United, the one against Hibs and then the penalty against Rangers. Although with the Rangers one, I was thinking to myself, 'I've maybe just poked a bear here: we play them in four days in the Scottish Cup and they've got five or six players coming back in to play!'

The 1-1 draw certainly sent Saints to Ibrox in good heart. What followed over the ensuing 120 minutes and beyond will never be forgotten by anyone of a Perth persuasion.

Guy Melamed

Each game in the Scottish Cup seemed to be more crazy than the previous game. They should make a movie of the quarter-final against Rangers. That was just crazy. It was like no game I have ever played in.

David Wotherspoon

To play against a team that was unbeaten in the league, and had lost once in the cup, was going to take a massive performance. We knew we needed to hang on as much as we could; they were going to get chances. It was about keeping them at bay as much as we were able and try and hit on the counter, or nick a goal at some point.

Callum Davidson

Going into the game at Ibrox, everyone said 'it's Rangers,

Rangers'. During the game, I thought we actually played quite well. Rangers had a few chances, but not many clear-cut chances. We had a couple of chances too.

Saints were given plenty of encouragement to advance on Allan McGregor's goal. The Gers' No. 1 had to make a fine save as Tanser connected with a first-time volley after Craig pulled a corner back to the edge of the box. At the other end, Alfredo Morelos fired over from close range, with the only other big chance created before the break seeing Filip Helander flick on Borna Barisic's out-swinging corner.

Zander Clark

We had played them in midweek and got such a positive result after a good performance. We went into the cup game with nothing to fear. We were fully aware that they hadn't lost at Ibrox all season (domestically), but we were confident that we could go there and cause an upset. We were under the cosh, I made a few saves, but we had chances ourselves.

Morelos then wasted two opportunities after the break – first heading a James Tavernier cross against a post before seeing Clark come up with a stunning save to deny his next effort. Saints sub, O'Halloran, almost snatched it, but saw two attempts blocked. The McDiarmid men had Clark to thank again for making it into extra time as he pulled off stops from Scott Wright and Kemar Roofe.

Craig Bryson

We had a game plan, we stuck to it and it worked. We have a belief in this team and we never know when we are beaten. We fought to the end.

Jamie McCart

The gaffer's been brilliant. I think the best thing I can say is that, tactically, everyone knows what they need to do when they go into a game. Like the Rangers cup game, we actually went and pressed them. We went in high up, we didn't just sit in. I think that was the most pleasing thing, especially for all the people watching.

Davidson had certainly been brave at Ibrox. With Craig operating behind Wotherspoon and McCann for defensive protection, it allowed the latter two to push up against Joe Aribo and Glen Kamara. May and Melamed led the line.

Zander Clark

When Morelos hit the post, it was weird. You just get that sort of thought in your head that this could actually be our night here.

David Wotherspoon

We dug in, used our substitutions, got it to extra time and just tried to keep going.

Michael O'Halloran

I came on in the 75th minute. It's strange, there are times you just get a feeling, and I remember before I came on, sat watching it, I just had an odd feeling. I remember I got it when we won the cup in 2014, and then I got it at the League Cup Final, sitting watching it. I thought, 'this is there for us'. I thought we played extremely well. Nobody really gave us a chance, and I think that kind of helped us a bit, because we went there with a freedom. Sometimes when you go there, you have to sit and then contain it, but we went out, I felt, and we played. We had some good chances and then, obviously, the more it went on, the more I felt, 'this is it'.

Extra time was typically tense. The league champions thought they had snatched it in the 117th minute as Tavernier bolted forward to head home Aribo's cross. The noise from the home bench suggested the importance of the goal, seemingly then crushing the dreams of Saints fans watching and listening at home.

Callum Davidson

As extra time was going on, I thought 'do we push, do we press?' The second period of extra time we started to get stronger, I thought we started to be the team controlling the game. Then they scored and I thought 'I can't believe it, after the effort we have put into it'.

Steven MacLean

We were drawing 0-0, did so well, and then Tavernier scored. I was gutted, given the work the players had put in. I felt so disappointed for them.

David Wotherspoon

When I was sitting on the bench (subbed on 71 minutes for Bryson), it was demoralising a wee bit. Having put in all that effort, to concede so late on was devastating.

Liam Craig

You could see from the reaction when Tavernier scored just how much it meant to their bench.

Zander Clark

When it went to extra time, we knew we were right in it. The boys were looking fresh and to lose the goal in the 117th minute, the boys could easily have crumbled and thought 'that's it'. But the spirit and the belief within everyone was superb. I remember getting the ball out of the net and kicking it up to the halfway line and saying, 'we'll create another chance'. Which we did . . . which led to the carnage . . .

Michael O'Halloran

Even losing the late goal, I remember going back to the centre, saying, 'there's a chance for us'. I mean, I remember looking at them and thinking they looked a wee bit dead on their feet.

With the time ticking past the allotted 120 minutes, Saints launched one final attack. Ex-Rangers forward O'Halloran was at the heart of it.

David Wotherspoon

For the boys to bounce back, guys making an impact off the bench, it was incredible. That is what Michael did. He played a massive part in the goal. Taking the ball in the last few moments and driving down the line, past a couple of players and getting a corner for the team was massive. It gets overshadowed by the goal and the celebrations after it, but that was a massive part in the game.

Liam Craig

When we win the ball back at our corner flag we don't just launch it, we actually play out from the back. We work it well in our half and Jamie ends up shanking it to the other side. Mikey gets on it and has his run, he does brilliantly.

Jamie McCart

I tried to play it to Mikey, but I didn't try to do it the way it happened. I was trying to play it near him, and then it just came to Shaun. I think we were all knackered, so I tried to play it but I shanked it, and it worked out perfectly, as from there Mikey won us the corner.

Michael O'Halloran

It went to Shaun, and your first initial thought is, 'get it in the box, time's running out,' but I remember standing next to him, and I was kind of free, and I was like, 'just give me it', because I still felt relatively fresh. So luckily enough, he's played it, and my idea was 'do something, if it's a cross or a corner, or something'. I just went down the right, and luckily enough I got the corner. Obviously, the rest is history . . .

Craig rushed over to take the corner . . . with 122 minutes on the clock . . .

Liam Craig

I always remember going up to take the corner and I just thought 'give the boys something to attack, don't have it too high and don't hit the first man, put it in an area where they can go and attack it'.

Craig Bryson

Liam played the majority of the game that night and he has gone over to take a corner in the 122nd minute. Everyone talks about Zander and Kano, but Liam has had to put the ball in a really good area. If he takes a bad corner, hits the front man, it's game over.

Scott Tanser

When 'Tav' scored I thought that was it. I was deflated. There didn't seem to be enough time left. We had more than matched Rangers but it was going to be tough to come back from that. But the way it happened was unbelievable.

David Wotherspoon

The rest speaks for itself! Liam's ball was just tremendous, right on point.

On their way! Jason Kerr leaps to net the crucial opening goal against Hibs in the Betfred League Cup semi-final. *Graeme Hart*

Shaun Rooney heads home Craig Conway's corner to win the Betfred League Cup against Livingston. *Graeme Hart*

Hampden hero! Shaun Rooney slides in celebration after his winner over Livi. *Graeme Hart*

Silverware scenes! St Johnstone lift the Betfred League Cup for the first time in their history! *Graeme Hart*

Unbelievable! Zander Clark flicks on Liam Craig's corner during late drama in the Scottish Cup quarter-final at Rangers. *Graeme Hart*

Icons at Ibrox! Zander leads the celebrations after Chris Kane knocked in the equaliser. *Graeme Hart*

Chris Kane steers home the opening goal in the Scottish Cup semi-final against St Mirren. *Graeme Hart*

The 32nd minute man! Shaun Rooney is the matchwinner again to defeat Hibs in the Scottish Cup Final. *Graeme Hart*

(L-R) David Wotherspoon, Michael O'Halloran and Stevie May –
three-time cup medal winners with St Johnstone. *Graeme Hart*

Captain fantastic! Jason Kerr savours the double-winning moments. *Graeme Hart*

Liam Gordon leads the celebrations back at McDiarmid Park. *Graeme Hart*

The trophy wait is over for Liam Craig, a double winner. *Graeme Hart*

Perth pride for (L-R) Steve Brown, Callum Davidson and Geoff Brown. *Graeme Hart*

Make Mine A Double, Callum! *Graeme Hart*

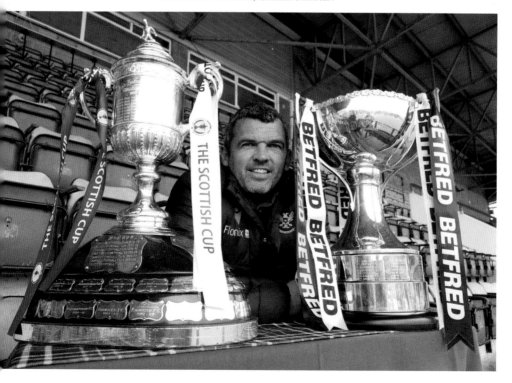

A club effort! All smiles at McDiarmid Park. *Graeme Hart*

Of course, Craig had an extra target to aim for in the congested penalty area. Roaming free, in a bright green goalie top, Clark had raced up for his first corner in a St Johnstone shirt.

Michael O'Halloran

I've watched it back loads of times and it gives you goose bumps watching it back.

Callum Davidson

Zander was running up and nodded at me and I just sort of nodded back. I think that is something all goalies do anyway. If there were five minutes to go, I would have stopped him, but because it was the last minute, up he went. People forget about what good quality the ball was. It's like Craig Conway in the cup final, right on the money. Rangers were unbeaten at Ibrox. They had a phenomenal season, and all credit to them.

Zander Clark

It's the first time I've done it at Saints. I remember doing it at Queen of the South, when I was on loan. We were 1-0 down at Hearts and I went up in the last minute, got my head to it and hit the outside of the post. I've probably always fancied being an aerial threat! I sometimes give the look over and get the 'nah, leave it, you just be the last line of defence'. That night at Ibrox I thought 'if we don't do anything, it's not as if they are going to break away up the park in a hurry to score a second'. It was last chance saloon for us. I thought I may as well go and see what happens. Little did I know what would unfold after that . . .

What drama followed. Nobody picked Clark up. He was, incredibly, allowed to wander into the six-yard box unmarked and head-flick on Craig's corner for Kane to memorably bundle home. The keeper proved just as handy in the opposition box as in his own.

Liam Craig

Zander came up and just stood there. Even watching it back now, you can't watch without laughing because there is just a big green person standing in the middle of their six-yard box with nobody near him. A lot of credit has to go to Kano, because he initially stops McGregor coming, and his movement is fantastic. That is the sort of thing Macca has worked on with Kano so much, drifting into areas where he can score goals. I knew right away something had happened after Zander had headed it, knew it had hit something else. It was just incredible. Again, it just sums up that whole squad, to be losing a goal at Ibrox in the 117th minute and still believing we will get one more opportunity. Zander does so well just to get enough on his header.

Paul Mathers

I remember seeing Zander at the halfway line and in he went. I think it was me and Macca, and we said 'nobody is picking him up'. I remember looking at Steven Gerrard and expecting him to be shouting something. I thought if it goes onto Zander, Allan McGregor is coming to punch it. But the rest is history. It's actually very clever. If you think about the amount of times goalkeepers go up for corner kicks, invariably 99% of the time they go and stand in with the four centre halfs and the four attackers. The biggest difference for me was that he just stood in the middle of the six-yard box. Up until then, I hadn't seen that. Liam's description is great as he just saw this great big boy with a big head, a beard and a bright green top. It was a great target for him.

Zander Clark

I knew our defenders, Jason, Jamie and Liam, would all be sort of bunched together at the corner, so my thought going up was to stand in the middle of the six-yard box and I'll take a player off them and leave them free. I've had it against me when a goalie comes up and it is bedlam, because nobody knows what to do.

I was surprised to be free. There wasn't a big commotion and no-one was in a hurry to pick me up. They seemed happy enough with me just standing there. Heading isn't my forte, but it was brilliant from Kano, a typical striker to be in and around that area. When we do set plays the day before games, I always say to the strikers 'get yourself in front of the goalkeeper and don't move'. If you are in the width of the posts, the amount of wee tap-in goals you can pick up is incredible. Thankfully, he found himself in that area and managed to toe-poke it in.

Chris Kane

I was on the goal edge to start with, that's where the manager usually puts me, on the goal edge, trying to stop him (the goalkeeper) coming and collecting the ball. But when you've got big Zander in the box, I think somebody has to go and mark him at least. Nobody did, that's the crazy thing.

Yeah, I start on the keeper and then when the ball comes in, as long as the keeper doesn't come to collect it, that's when I move to the back post. I try to create some space if the ball comes through and lands there – which it did. Barisic was holding me as well, which kind of helped me, because if he isn't holding me, he could probably go and kick the ball away or something. Zander jumps up and heads it. It bounces, kind of falls down to my foot, hits my foot and goes in. But I honestly wasn't bothered who got the goal, whether it was me or if it was Zander. It was an unbelievable moment and I don't think any St Johnstone fan will ever forget it, really. I'll never forget it, anyway.

Clark wheeled away in utter jubilation – it seemed nobody could catch him.

Chris Kane

Just to see Zander running away, all the boys falling on him, it was absolutely crazy. I actually had to watch it back a few times to see if it did hit me!

Callum Davidson

Probably one of my most enjoyable moments in football was big Zander just nodding his head going up the pitch, standing in the middle of the six-yard box, free, and knocking it in. Well, he doesn't knock it in! He runs away and Jason tries to jump on him and he just chucks him off. Kano is running behind him going 'it's my goal, it's my goal.' It was brilliant, that's when you miss supporters. If you had St Johnstone fans at the game, what an incredible memory. I think that is why we all play and watch football – for that type of memory.

Steven MacLean

It was unbelievable! The joy, the excitement, the sort of disbelief, as I couldn't believe what had happened. I hadn't realised that Kano had put it in. I thought it was Zander until someone said. My son showed me the celebration of me and Callum going mental, which is now good to see.

David Wotherspoon

Zander is a big guy. He always wants to come up for corners late in a game and is always looking at the bench thinking 'can I go up? Can I go up?' He got his opportunity. He went, made himself big, his presence was felt and they didn't pick him up. I feel like he should have done better with the header, but he made contact with it and directed it towards goal – that's what matters. It ended up in the back of the net and Kano was in the right position just to tap it in. It was a huge celebration. It was something very special. You felt we were on a roll.

Guy Melamed

When Zander went up for the corner and we scored I remember the reaction of Steven Gerrard. He was so shocked. I had come off before extra-time. I was so happy and jumping around when Zander ran past the Rangers bench. It was mad. They were a fine team and went on to be champions. But Rangers faced a St Johnstone team which was the best in the whole history of the club.

Zander Clark

I knew it had hit somebody, I wasn't sure who. I thought it had hit Kano. But I couldn't have cared if Kano had flicked it up and done three keepie-ups and volleyed it in, I was off. I was milking it. It was just that joy of equalising in the last minute and we've got a chance now in the lottery of a penalty shoot-out.

Chris Kane

I was just running with the boys a little bit, and I couldn't care who it hit and went in, but I made sure afterwards in the changing room that all the boys knew it hit off me! I made sure they knew that. Zander was still trying to claim it!

I had to watch it at least 20 times that night! I've watched it a lot more than that now. You do need to watch it back and watch it in slow-motion and stuff, just to see exactly what's happened, and it was just phenomenal, really, just the whole game. Especially going down with a couple of minutes to go, you're thinking, 'that's us beat', but that's obviously what we were like all season. We just never give up, and it showed. Obviously, it was one of my best games that I can ever remember.

Paul Mathers

When it happened, you think Zander has scored. I felt sorry for

Kano. It's the first time I've seen a goal scorer actually chasing somebody who is celebrating his goal!

Michael O'Halloran
I remember Zander took off. I was just at the six-yard box, I had a straight-on view of the goal, and there was just a feeling of relief. Then he's gone! Where's he got that energy from?

If the script seemed written for Clark to go on and be the penalty shoot-out hero, Saints' immediate task was to keep calm and find five spot-kick takers. Conway, May, Melamed and Wotherspoon – all likely candidates – weren't on the park. Craig was perhaps the only recognised name to strike from 12 yards.

Liam Craig
I remember walking over to Macca. I took the fifth penalty against Dunfermline, and he was like 'are you going fifth?' I said, 'No, I'll go first, because looking about here, there's not many penalty-takers on the park: we might not get as far as fifth.'

Jason Kerr
After we scored, I was thinking ahead to the penalties and I was like, 'I really want to take one.' I was straight up to the gaffer and Mac, like, 'I want to take one, I want to take one!' 'Who wants to take one?' said Macca. 'Aye, Mac, Mac!' He kept on writing all the names down. 'Mac! I'll take one!' and then he says, 'Ah, I'll let you take one.'

Steven MacLean
It was funny when we went to see who was going to take the penalties – the boys were just so excited at what had just happened. It was hard trying to calm them down a little bit. It

was so surreal, mad! Jason kept saying 'Macca, I'll take one, I'll take one.' I kept looking elsewhere . . .

Chris Kane

I was on the fifth penalty. I put my name first, so I looked to go first, and then Liam Craig overruled me and he said, 'No, I'll take first,' so I just swapped with him, as he was meant to be fifth. I was putting my name forward for the limelight on the fifth pen!

Tavernier went straight down the middle with the first kick, and Clark stood firm to palm it away with his right hand.

Zander Clark

Tavernier had taken so many penalties and there was so much footage. I think there are maybe 40 clips of penalties and you're going 'how are you meant to work out anything from this?' Thankfully, I think his most recent ones went the way I go to dive. I don't know if I move early or what, and he sort of changes his mind, and I manage to get a strong hand on it. It's obviously a bonus if you can save the first one and then go up and score your first. We did it in the quarter-finals as well at Dunfermline. It gives you the ascendancy.

Craig, Barisic and Booth then all slotted home, all with their left foot. Jermain Defoe found the bottom left corner for 2-2, before up stepped Kerr . . .

Chris Kane

Obviously, seeing big 'Jase' stepping up, I thought, 'Oh, no, he's a centre-half, where's he putting this?' and he wellied it right in the top corner!

Jason Kerr

I think everyone I spoke to, I asked, 'How did you feel when I was taking a penalty?' They were like, 'well . . .' I think even all the Rangers fans were probably thinking I was going to miss it. I did feel the minute I put that ball down on the penalty spot I was just going to smash it, and I don't think I actually meant for it to go that high, but it obviously went into the top left corner.

Allan McGregor was giving me a bit (of chat), the ball was just down in the ring beside him, and I walked right up to him, and he was like, 'sorry, mate'. 'No bother,' I said. I put the ball on the deck and just smashed it and gave him a wee look, and that was a good moment for me again.

Steven MacLean

Jason's penalty was unbelievable actually, so fair play to him.

Clark carried on his superman act by pushing away Roofe's effort down to his left.

Paul Mathers

We had done our stuff for the penalty shoot-out. Zander helped get the equaliser, but when it came to the penalties he was quite calm. He had come back to reality and was focused on the penalties. On the Tavernier one, I basically said 'listen, he has had about 40-odd penalties and I haven't got a clue which side he is going to'. But I said 'just don't go too early, stand as long as you can'. As Roofe is stepping up, Zander is looking across at me at the dug-out. If he ever forgets, then I've got to give him a signal as to which way we think he is going. We got that one right, from the work we do on a continual basis. If you look back at the night, he saved two, and went the right way for another one. To do that at Rangers, and don't forget the Dunfermline game where he produced two saves out of the five, has been pleasing from the goalkeeping department.

Zander Clark

We had done our homework on them all. You can watch as many clips as you want, but if they step up and decide they are going another way you have no chance. I think Barisic changed from what he usually does. We knew Defoe hit it low, hard in that corner, but I was at full stretch and it beat me. If they strike the ball cleanly enough, the reaction time from 12 yards is pretty slim. With Jason's penalty, if you smash it like that, nine times out of 10, it's not coming back.

McCann held his nerve to beat McGregor at the bottom left and end Rangers' double hopes in a thrilling penalty shoot-out victory. Saints were heading back to Hampden. Cue euphoria.

Ali McCann

Liam (Craig) was giving me a bit of grief the whole week practising penalties. When I was walking up, someone said 'he missed all his penalties in training, we're definitely in trouble here'. I was confident enough in the end. I saved my penalty for the important one!

We didn't have many recognised penalty-takers left. I was quite happy at number four, as I said I would take one. I thought 'how bad can it be?' I went up and it worked out perfectly in the end. I think we had two chances to win it, so for me it was the least pressure I could really have. I tried to put it where I was trying to in training and thankfully it went in, even though the keeper went the right way.

Chris Kane

Obviously, we scored our penalties and it took the pressure off me a wee bit, and then Zander came up with a few brilliant saves.

Steven MacLean

The boys were a different class in the penalty shoot-out. Paul Mathers was like 'who was after that, Macca?' I showed him the list and he was like 'oh, just as well we won it 4-2!'

Jamie McCart

I was the next one after, number six, so I was glad it finished when it did! The standard of the penalties was incredible, wasn't it? Allan McGregor didn't get any of them, which was a surprise, because he's an incredible goalkeeper.

Michael O'Halloran

The quality of the penalties from us was ridiculous! Ridiculous! Zander, too, stepped up to make the two big saves. I just felt after that, a feeling throughout the dressing room, that we were going to keep going on – we were really confident. A few of the Rangers staff congratulated me and wished me all the best in the next round, so that was a nice touch.

Scott Tanser

I will never forget that Rangers game. But when everyone was celebrating, I was in a treatment room by myself watching the game on a monitor. I had rolled my ankle badly and had to come off. We put everything into that game. That performance against a Rangers team that didn't lose to a Scottish side at Ibrox all season was up there with our very best.

It was mayhem but I was celebrating sat on a bed by myself when the penalties were going in. I couldn't walk out even to look on. I'd have put my name down to take a penalty. Thankfully, they all kept calm and got the job done.

Little moments can encapsulate an entire season. If Clark hadn't flicked on for the last-gasp leveller at Ibrox, if Saints hadn't won the penalty shoot-out at Dunfermline or if Middleton hadn't scored against Ross County for the top six, dreams would have been over. Sometimes it's meant to be.

Callum Davidson

To win the shoot-out, the penalties were fantastic from us. It would have been such a blow to score in the last minute, get a deserved draw I would say in the game, then to lose on penalties; it would have been harsh. It was a brilliant, brilliant night. I was buzzing, delighted. When we scored, I thought 'we have a chance to create something big'. I tried to keep it within myself, not let the players realise it. But I knew something huge could happen.

David Wotherspoon

Anything can happen in a penalty shoot-out and the pressure was back on them. We had nothing to lose. The boys stuck the penalties away so well and the big man, again, added to so many massive saves over the season. He is a big guy in penalties. When you step up against him, you are sort of worrying a wee bit.

When you look at Liam, Callum and Jason stepping up to take their penalties, they all just put them away so well. Jason's penalty was tremendous, just caught it so well. And Ali, so much pressure on him for a young boy, he just slotted it away like he does all the time. It was just tremendous and the celebrations after it were amazing. It was huge that night and I think that just pushed us towards everything else at the end of the season.

Given Clark's heroics, social media went crazy – Zander was trending.

Zander Clark

I've got a group chat with my brother and my mates and they were forwarding all the clips on from social media. They were buzzing off it, it was a good laugh.

Chris Kane

It wasn't just the equaliser, it was the whole game, the fact we had beaten Rangers. Social media went mad. There were hundreds and hundreds of messages that I got, and obviously you can't reply to them all, but you just need to thank all the fans for everything they've done. They've stuck with us, sending us all messages the whole season, it's been great.

Alistair Stevenson

Zander played in the youth team and he was always so big, he had such potential. I think he really flourished when he went out on loan, adult football so to speak, and it became more of a challenge for him. He was always a great shot-stopper and is a great character. He won many a game for you just by the saves he made.

Stevie May

I was obviously in the same youth team as Zander, so I've known him for years. We went on holiday together to Ibiza when we were 16 or 17, we played on loan, he was at Elgin, I was at Alloa, and we played against each other, and then we go full circle and come back and play in the team again. With the boys who have been here before, it's almost like nothing has changed since the first time. Obviously, when you're younger, you never think that will happen.

Elliott Parish

It's not difficult at all to enjoy it with Zander. The big man is a great guy and he deserves every plaudit he gets. I'm nothing but thrilled for him, if I'm honest. There is no difficulty seeing someone like that do well. It's a great club to be a part of.

Alex Cleland

It was a special night. The two games we played against Rangers were very, very close. I think they knew it wasn't going to be easy playing against us, especially because of the way we play and we are hard to play against. We were in good form, as they were, an excellent side. We knew we had to be at our best, as did they. Zander had some brilliant saves and we maybe rode our luck a little, but we played well and kept going. To get the goal at the end was superb. Over the two games, we were a good match for Rangers, who were flying at that time, chasing the title and the double as well. Not many teams have taken anything off Rangers. To get that penalty shoot-out win was brilliant.

Paul Mathers

People forget that was our second game against Rangers in four days and it was the second time we had fought back. That is when you give the boys real credit. For us to come back against Rangers twice in four days, to draw one and then beat them on penalties, it shows the incredible mentality of the players.

Callum Hendry

Going to Aberdeen was, personally, the best thing I'd done – I needed to go and play. I needed a different experience, so it was good to go there and get some games, get some goals. But I always kept an eye on Saints. My best pals are here, so it was important that I watched all the games. I was watching the Rangers match, and I couldn't believe it. I could not believe it happened! Going on loan, that's football. I love this club and it's a great set of boys here. I wanted to watch the boys and make sure they did well, which they did.

Craig Bryson

I think a lot of the players inside that night were thinking 'is this written in the stars for us now?' That effectively was a final for us, going to Ibrox, with nothing to lose. With the teams left in the competition, we felt we had as good a chance as anyone and we had the experience of Hampden with the Betfred Cup behind us. I think that night we thought 'maybe something special is going to happen here'.

Jamie McCart

Even now after winning the Scottish Cup, I just look back to that game and I think that was one of the best games. No one gave us a shot. They were unbeaten in the league, they thought they were going to win the double. Then to go there and do that was phenomenal.

Callum Davidson

I think it's a big thing for me, when people look back at our success, that we beat one of the Old Firm to get there.

A Scottish Cup semi-final with St Mirren was just 14 days away.

SEVEN

THE BELIEVERS

'We had a back four, what with a combined age of about 200 or something (!), but we just knew our jobs. This defensive group are younger, in their 20s, and are getting better all the time.'
Dave Mackay, 2014 Scottish Cup-winning Captain

Using the title of a previous club book, Saints were simply 'bristling with possibilities' at the business end of the season. With one trophy in the cabinet, the club was now chasing the Scottish Cup and European qualification to continue a dream season. That sentence alone seemed mind boggling for even the most optimistic supporter.

Yet such was Davidson's faith and confidence in his tight-knit squad, he made seven changes for the league trip to Easter Road – clearly with one eye on the semi-final with St Mirren. His players responded to the call, as on-loan Middleton capitalised on a mistake in the first half and a well-oiled defensive machine held firm for a priceless three points.

Glenn Middleton
I scored early on against Hibs and I was confident, but it all built from the first day when everyone was so positive towards me.

They made me feel comfortable at the club and I could look to express myself on the pitch.

In another change in Edinburgh, Parish came in for Clark (toe injury) to make his first league appearance since September. Together with the regular, consistent back three performers, he kept Hibs at bay to go fifth in the table ahead of Livingston on goal difference. It continued a remarkable run of form in 2021.

Paul Mathers

For Elliott to come in and play at Hibs, and keep a clean sheet, when he hadn't played in the league for so long, it shows you how hard he works.

Elliott Parish

I tried hard to help us win the cups and finish where we did in the league. I was fortunate, at the end of the season, to play against Hibs and be a part of a vital 1-0 win and almost secure fifth spot. A draw would have been great, to go into that final Livingston game needing a win, but we ended up beating Hibs to give us some breathing space. It was nice to play a part, in that respect.

The Saints' train was firmly on track, picking up a head of steam as it reeled in Livi in the quest for another European journey. Suddenly, though, it was derailed. Covid hit.

6 May 2021 Newsflash . . .
'Four St Johnstone players to miss semi-final after two positive Covid-19 tests' (BBC online)

Three days before the semi-final, the news broke. Two players had tested positive for Covid-19 – with another two ruled out through test-and-trace measures. Craig, Davidson, May and Parish all missed out at Hampden.

Liam Craig
It was horrible, given I was thinking I had another chance of playing in a semi-final.

Elliott Parish
It was just about how many of the boys ended up going down with it at that stage of the season. It was carnage. It was an unsettling time.

Callum Davidson
I was missing four massive players, especially Liam and Muzz, two major parts of the midfield. Again, for Muzz, it was heartbreaking as he has missed big games. He was desperate to get back.

Murray Davidson
I missed out after being deemed to be a close contact of one of the lads with Covid. I couldn't believe that. It was really hard to accept and you feel so helpless looking on.

Callum Davidson
It is something that is so hard to deal with. I'm not a stressful person, don't really get too stressed about many things, and it was the one thing I was really stressed about, because I was having to make decisions not just for players on the pitch, but for families which affected other people. It was virtually my decision, while having help from the medical staff. We had to make decisions based on the advice we were given. To lose the players was hard enough, but to have them not train was tough. If you don't train as a professional athlete for 10 days, it has a huge effect on your body. If people are isolating with Covid, it's

difficult to come back with the same energy levels. After you are ill, you can go back to work, but you have to run about the pitch for 90 minutes as well.

Liam Craig

The reason we were so successful in regard to Covid is because everyone bought into the protocols that the club were adopting. You couldn't go to a restaurant, sit and have a coffee, you couldn't go anywhere. Nobody could have envisaged the pandemic that we've been through, but from a player's point of view, the club couldn't have done any more in terms of looking after the players and their welfare, not just during that period, but during the whole season. I had taken all the right precautions, as had the club and my family. It was just one of those things that happened and there was no getting away from it.

It was hardly ideal preparation for the meeting with St Mirren, but Saints – not for the first time – sought to dig deep and win for their absent team-mates. The Buddies, though, were seeking a first Scottish Cup semi-final victory since they last won the competition in 1987.

Callum Davidson

We had only finished ahead of them on goal difference to get into the top six. They had lost in the League Cup semi-final to Livingston, so we knew they were hungry. I thought it was going to be a pretty even game.

David Wotherspoon

I felt like we were expected to win the game, given the form we were in. I felt that pressure. I felt the pressure was on us – and it was tough.

After a bright Saints start, featuring efforts from Rooney and Kane,

St Mirren could have taken the lead on the half-hour mark. Kristian Dennis's cushioned volley found Lee Erwin, but somehow Clark was able to keep it out from point-blank range.

David Wotherspoon

We had that scare when Zander made an unbelievable save from Erwin. He always pops up at the right times with the big saves. These little things can change your mindset or give you the confidence to push on and win the game.

Zander Clark

The ball came across the six-yard box and I just managed to get a hand on it.

The sides continued to trade blows after the break, with Ilkay Durmus forcing a stop out of Clark before Wotherspoon curled an effort just wide. Durmus then gave substitute Collin Quaner a chance he couldn't take. Middleton, though, was ready to make his mark, replacing Melamed on 65 minutes.

Callum Davidson

We played really well. I thought we actually moved the ball really well and had really good composure. Glenn came on and produced a couple of moments of magic, which is basically why I brought him in.

In a flowing 72nd-minute move down the left, featuring a nutmeg from McCann, Booth found Middleton whose left-footed centre was perfectly weighted for Kane to flick home with his right foot into the far corner. It was a typical No.9's finish.

Callum Davidson

We work on the front players staying in the middle. I think

Kano is doing that more and more. I think his performances last season for me were probably the best I've seen him. Kano, for me, has been one of our best players improvement-wise. It was a great ball by Glenn for the goal, it was a great move. Callum Booth was out of the team and came in. He was unbelievable.

Ali McCann

It was a move that started at the back and then I saw a few guys around and just tried to flick it through. It does look quite satisfying on the video watching it back. It turned out quite nice, it was a great move. I slipped it to Callum, then into Glenn and then into Kano. It was a move that went all the way through the team. I didn't expect the nutmeg to look so clean to be fair, I was just hoping!

Callum Booth

For the goal, I've made the run from our own box and Ali's played it into my path and I've run on, so yeah, it was a good move and a good goal from us.

I used to be a really attacking full-back, a guy who always wanted to go forward. I suppose, as time goes on and you get a little bit more experienced, and probably a little bit older and slower, I've started maybe using my experience a little bit more and just going at certain times. I still like to get forward, still feel that I'm relatively fit and can get up and down, and the gaffer likes me to do that, to play the different formations.

Hampden was good, a big, massive pitch, so I liked playing there; it kind of suited me. I tend to get forward in the second half more as games open up and my fitness can come through a little. So yeah, in that semi-final especially I was kind of getting forward a fair bit, even against Hibs in the final as well. I've definitely still got a few more years left in me, I would like to think, to do that.

It was just good, I suppose, to get in the team. I mean, around Christmas, January time, I think I was on the bench maybe six games in a row, but you always know that football can change so quickly, and it only takes one little injury, or a little bit of loss of form to get you a place in the team. The games were coming thick and fast, and just getting that run in the team helped me. I remember crossing for Rooney's header against Celtic in February and I kicked on.

Steven MacLean

Every day we will work on different things with the strikers. If there is work to be done there with them, I normally do it, but it is a collective thing as well and I'm always speaking to Callum and Alex. If you look at Kanos' goals over the years, he doesn't score goals from 20 yards out, he scores them in the penalty box, most strikers do. You do get strikers that score from distance, but he needs to be in the box to score goals. We're always looking to help them and make them aware of different things. Chris does so much work for the team and sometimes he needs to probably be a bit more selfish and get in the box more. The work he does for the team is incredible and that is why he has played a lot of games. Even when he didn't score, he was still contributing a lot. I'm delighted for the players, individually and as a team. We are a big group that wants success, it's not just about individuals.

Alistair Stevenson

The way Chris played last season is the way I remember him as a 17-year-old youth team player. He was your match-winner, he put himself all over the pitch up front. He would chase balls, run into channels, win you corners, force keepers into saves and always wanted to take the penalty kicks. He has always been able to score goals and has just needed regular games. He is so much admired by his team-mates as he never stops working. He is phenomenal. When he comes off the pitch, he has always put so much into it. His confidence is now on a high and I think he is in a really good place.

Chris Kane

Yeah, obviously Macca was massive when I played with him, growing up, so for him to come back to the club was a massive bonus for me. I'm sure the other strikers think the same, because he takes you for drills after training. All the other boys, defenders and midfielders, they might be going in, but he'll keep the strikers behind and it's just working on little things. You might not think that affects your own game, but it really does. I've noticed that myself, the wee bits I've been doing, it's just like what he's been taking us for after training, so he has been massive coming back in.

It was a very important goal against St Mirren. That's what Macca is always telling me to do: get even just a wee yard or two ahead, just get in front of the man. I just slid in, got a toe on it, and obviously it went into the bottom corner. It's wee movements like that he's always telling me to do. It's the easiest thing for defenders to mark you if you're just standing still, so it's these wee movements that I've been trying to work on to get a yard or two of space.

As we've tried keeping the same system, we've had a few wee changes up front, but you do work on it in training a lot so you know where the boys are going to run and how they're going to be putting the ball in. I tell them myself – if they get a space, whip it in and I'll try to get across the front or at the back.

Two minutes later Middleton made it 2-0 with a sumptuous free-kick from 25 yards. What a purple patch.

Callum Davidson

Glenn's free-kick was something special. I remember watching it and as soon as he hit it, I went 'that's in'. The goalie didn't move, such was the pace he hit it with. To do it at Hampden, I was delighted for him. I signed him from Rangers, and he probably wasn't quite up to speed. Like with Guy, it was patience and knowing when to chuck him in. He was getting frustrated and I just felt he was getting better and better. Ultimately, he basically played himself into the final by his effort and work rate and realising where he had to be.

David Wotherspoon

I think the gaffer did that well over the season, introducing boys at the right times. Look at Glenn and what he did for the team when he came on as a sub. He scored the winner to get us into the top six towards the end of the game and then came on in the semi-final against St Mirren, looked lively and set up the first goal. Then he stepped up to take the free-kick. I think if Scott Tanser had been on the pitch, he might have been trying to take it! For him to step up and take it the way he did was tremendous, what a goal it was.

Glenn Middleton

I took a free-kick in the league game at Hibs and it went over the bar. I was raging with myself. Everyone was asking why I was so angry. But I practise these free-kicks a lot and I was disappointed with that one.

You have to make time to work on those skills yourself. When it pays off it means so much. When it came to the semi-final free-kick, there was no way anyone else was taking it! But the boys wouldn't have let me take it if they didn't respect me. You know if you have hit a golf ball purely and it is the same with free-kicks. You know if it's going in or if it's heading for Row Z. I knew right away I had hit it well. It was an unbelievable feeling when it went in to give us a two-goal lead. That is definitely the highlight of my career so far. It will take a lot to beat it.

When we were all celebrating at the corner flag it was one of those moments you wished would never end. The only thing that would have made it even better was if there had been fans there to share it with. Remember we had boys missing from that game because of Covid. I don't think people fully appreciate how that can affect a squad, the rhythm and build-up to the game. But once again it showed how united we were in that dressing room. Everyone backed each other.

Conor McCarthy headed in a late set-piece to make it a nervy finish, but Saints held on as a stunning double bid stayed alive.

Zander Clark

It was a sticky game and one where we were just glad to get the job done. They scored late on and it became a bombardment of the box, but the boys were incredible in terms of how we defended and just had that will and desire not to let them get another free header in the box.

Callum Davidson

The last 10 minutes against St Mirren, Lorna was telling me she was basically walking around the garden after they scored. I was actually quite comfortable, was okay at the side, I wasn't panicking too much. It was a big win and a really good performance.

David Wotherspoon

It was tremendous to do it. Again, it wasn't just the XI on the pitch, it was the boys coming off the bench who made an impact. We obviously conceded a goal, but we hung on.

Murray Davidson

The Scottish Cup semi-final was probably the most nervous I've ever been watching a game. Luckily the lads came through against St Mirren to reach another final and I was determined to make the squad. It would have been devastating to miss out on a third cup final.

If it had been a tense finish on the pitch, for Craig watching at home it was total agony.

Liam Craig

The semi-final was the worst for me. It was horrendous. I remember waking up, it must have been about half-six on the Sunday morning. Obviously, Hibs had beaten Dundee United in the other semi-final – which I was actually quite pleased about because all the pressure would be on Hibs in the final. The club had sorted me out with a spin bike, so I had that in the house, just to keep ticking over. So half-six I'm up, seven o'clock, I'm on that spin bike, just counting down the hours. Luckily, it was a two o'clock kick-off, and then I texted into the group, just a message wishing them all the best and all the rest of it. We were having some banter and everyone was laughing and joking, and I just felt there was a real relaxation about the squad.

Over the next couple of hours, I organised a Zoom call with a few of the boys that were missing, which was great. I had Zander's strip on, one of his goalie strips that he'd given me, for watching the game, the kids were buzzing for it. His number was 12, so that shows how old it was! I was just really getting into it, but feeling nervous, just because there's nothing you can do! I'd spoken to a few of the boys, I spoke to the skipper, spoke to Liam Gordon, spoke to Zander on the morning of the game, but there's nothing you can do. I texted the manager, texted Macca and I just felt, 'we're better than them, this is the first time in such a big game that we've been favourites'. There was nothing between us and Livi, and not a lot between us and St Mirren.

Watching the game, it was horrible. I had a few beers, and I knew it could go either way. But in the second half I felt as if we just stepped it up a gear. In both the semi-final and the final, it felt like the opposition had a good chance. Zander made a good save 20 minutes in or so, then we weathered it, and once we got the goal we were away.

As I say, it was one of the most horrible experiences of my life, my football life, anyway. When Kano scored, I was going absolutely mental, to the point where the neighbour across the road was out in her garden, looking across wondering 'what's happening in there?' because they probably never even knew St Johnstone were playing! And then Glenn's free-kick, when that went in, you just thought, 'that's it, we've done it, we've done it', and then when they scored, that was horrible, that five minutes, because you were thinking, 'they'll get a chance' – you always get a chance.

Then when big Liam went off, it might only have been for 20 seconds but it felt like a lifetime watching. I had a wee wobble! It was great to see it out and I thought Callum Booth was man of the match that day. I know everyone speaks of David Wotherspoon, but I felt 'Boothy' was exceptional in terms of how he played and how he actually linked with David.

It really cheered me up as it was a hard time, watching people going about their business, the world still going on, and you're stuck in the house with three kids, me and Laura. I said to Laura, 'I just need to get through to Thursday', because I wasn't getting out of isolation until then. To get back into training on the Thursday was just a huge relief, with the excitement of going to play against Livi, and then looking forward to the cup final the week after.

Davidson should have been savouring one of the best periods of his first year in management, preparing for the midweek trip to Celtic and the meeting with Livi to close out the league season. Instead, Covid was his biggest concern. He was struggling to even take a team to Glasgow.

Callum Davidson

I think it hit home, really, when we got it just towards the end of the season, how quickly it can spread. We had basically taken every precaution we possibly could and it just kept spreading. We had 10 players missing. For the Celtic game, we didn't have a goalie, had to play Charlie Gilmour, a young lad. I think I had Guy and David on the bench and the other two were kids. That's where we were with Celtic. It's probably the first time I've ever been delighted with a 4-0 defeat, just because of the pressure that was on us. We were still trying to finish fifth at the time. Livingston lost 3-0 to Rangers that night and I always knew the goal difference was a big thing. I knew a draw at home would clinch fifth for us and I had every confidence we would do that.

But just day to day, it was like 'who have I got to pick from? Have I got a team?' I had to get an emergency loan goalie, and big Bobby (Zlamal) came in. He is some man, and all thanks to him. But it was just a horrendous time. I remember saying to Lorna 'I should be really enjoying this time, because we are fighting at the top'. But it was probably one of the most stressful times I've ever had. When we had the outbreak, it was just basically walk in, train, leave work and go back home. I didn't do anything, just went back to my house. I think the players were the same, and you have to give them credit. It was a little bit of an eye opener. It was hard for the players. They didn't see anybody. I always remember thinking 'will I have a team for the cup final?' That was basically my biggest worry, 'who is going to be fit? Who will be able to cope? If they had Covid, can they replicate the energy levels?' We weren't able to train for two days between the semi-final and the Celtic game, weren't allowed to. We all had to get tested at 8.30pm on the Tuesday night at McDiarmid. The players had to travel from home and get tested. We had to get tested every two days, whereas other teams were once a week. We kept trying to break the chain. I understood health-wise, but for me trying to pick teams, who is fit, who is available, I didn't know. Trying to put a training session on was a challenge. Coming to the games, I couldn't work on anything, couldn't do anything and the players just went out and put a real shift in.

Zander Clark
With the final coming up, it was a worrying time. Everyone was wrapped up in cotton wool just to make sure we had a squad for the final. It was nerve-wracking. The manager must have been tearing his hair out, as it's the last thing you want with a game coming up to try and win the double. We had gone the full season with one or two, then to get nine players or so missing with Covid a week before the final, it must have been a headache for the manager. But, credit to the medical team; we managed to get everyone isolated who needed to be and back match fit. They supplied boys with exercise bikes and programmes to make sure we weren't losing out on the fitness side of things and we were ready to go.

Liam Craig
We had the game against Celtic on the Wednesday. At least there were games all the way through to keep me occupied. Trust me, when I was watching the Livi game, coinciding with our game, watching the goal difference, I'm just thinking to myself, 'can we just not concede another goal?'

Bobby Zlamal, Goalkeeper, 35
When I went to St Mirren in similar circumstances in September, Hearts were still in pre-season and I had played in a Friday night

friendly at Tynecastle at 6pm before I played against Hibs the next day. I had four games in seven days after a week of double sessions.

It was different when the call came from St Johnstone. I was ready for my holidays. I said 'yes' right away but I wasn't sure if my body was ready.

I had only one training session before playing against Celtic and even that was at a distance from the rest of the team because of Covid. I had to Google the names of some of the players but of course they have nicknames so that didn't help much on the pitch. But you are so involved in the game you don't have time to think of a player's name anyway. You can shout numbers.

We didn't have any time to talk about tactics. It was weird, but I am quite an experienced guy and told myself just not to do anything silly. We lost an early goal at Celtic and that didn't help. It was my first touch, I think. But it was very controversial. Jason Kerr was looking to pass to Shaun Rooney, not me. I was surprised when the referee gave a free-kick. The assistant didn't think it was a back pass either when I asked him.

If I had been with the team longer, I would have told the wall not to jump because the free-kick was so close or I'd have had a man lying on the ground. I was disappointed of course. I had a few good saves, but we lost so they didn't matter.

Steven MacLean

When Zander got injured and then with the Covid stuff, we were like 'who can we get?' Paul (Mathers) deals with all that and he and Callum came up with Zlamal, who was available. I knew Bobby from playing with him (at Hearts). Callum spoke to him and he said, 'Macca is crazy!' I said, 'Macca is not crazy any longer Bobby!' He is a great lad, such a great character. He came in and the boys loved him. He wanted to come to the final as well. The way the boys were with him was great. He is a top, top guy.

Paul Mathers

It was unfortunate, with the way Covid was going through the squad. If you only had one goalkeeper over the age of 21, you could go and get a loan. At that stage of the season, the manager felt it was a good move. Bobby was available. We actually went to Hearts and tried to sound out a couple of their goalkeepers, Craig Gordon being one. Bobby came in. We knew he was a real character through Macca, but he came in and we just treated him like he was one of ours. Even though he was only in for two weeks, I think he really enjoyed it. We work hard, but we have fun, it's relaxed and we get the job done. The Celtic game was quite hard for him as he hadn't played for a while, or trained that much either, and obviously we were down to the bare bones.

Elliott Parish

I was watching the Celtic game at home and was just watching the goal difference in the league. Rangers were playing Livingston at the time, and we almost equalled their result. It was probably one of the best 4-0 losses St Johnstone have ever had in the end, which is crazy isn't it really?

Charlie Gilmour, Midfielder, 22

It was nice to come in (at Celtic). The team was playing well before I arrived (in February) and then when I got here. But hopefully I can work my way into the team and be a big, important player for the club.

Callum Davidson

Getting Liam, Mayso and Muzz back for the Livi game and others the following Wednesday before the cup final was the first time I had an indication of my team. You think about your cup-final preparations, working out your plans, it's great, it's this and that, but it was horrendous as I didn't have half the team. It was then deciding, of the ones who had had it, can they play? Who can play? For the Betfred Cup Final, I knew the team really, but Wednesday, Thursday, even getting to Friday, I still didn't know, as I had to watch players in training to see how they were. It was a really difficult decision. It was totally different to the 2014 Scottish Cup Final build-up, that's for sure.

Liam Craig

The first day back for me was the toughest. That Thursday before the Saturday, with the sweat coming out of you. On the Friday I felt a wee bit normal again, but 20 minutes into the Livingston game me and Muzz were looking at each other a bit worried!

Bobby Zlamal

Before the Livingston game I had a chance to train more and get to know the team. I thought it would be a close match. It was quite a boring game, but I knew I would have one or two saves to make and I was pleased with the one when I used my legs to block the shot from Jaze Kabia in the second half. After losing to Celtic, I was happy to help the team get the result needed to get them into Europe.

Steven MacLean

Bobby did well for us, making that great save against Livi to help us achieve that top five. There were so many key moments in the season.

Paul Mathers

A lot of people won't remember that save against Livi. It wasn't a spectacular one, but it was important. Bobby also did a couple of other things in that game that he made look easy. The point that he helped us win that day was massive.

Callum Davidson

I think the players believed in what we were doing. They had every confidence they could win any game of football. The record from January was incredible.

The battling 0-0 draw with Livi sealed fifth spot and a European ticket – for the first time since 2017 – by just two goals. Take a bow the Perth Saints.

Liam Craig

We're still a young squad, and a few of the older ones have maybe been there and done it, so it was up to us to drive those standards forward. What we've got at St Johnstone is a great group of younger players, wanting to learn. Ali McCann, Jason Kerr, none of them are big-headed or arrogant, they want to do as well as they can for the club and for themselves. When you then bring in Craig Bryson, who's been honestly incredible in the way he trains and the way he works, Craig Conway, another one, 36 years old but comes in with goals and assists, it's great for the young lads to look up to these guys. I put myself in there as well, guys 34 and 35 years old, and look how they train, look how they look after themselves and look how they demand standards are set.

Steven MacLean

It becomes a habit, when you keep winning. We found a way to win playing well, and even when we didn't play well we picked up results, which is a great trait to have too. We played well at the start of the season but we couldn't get over the line at times. From January to the end of the season, we just got on a run.

Scott Tanser

Things just clicked and we were flying. We had an unbelievable end to the season.

EIGHT

DOWN TO THE WIRE

'It's down to the wire. Rising up, gonna' be a star.'
Skyfoss
(2021 Scottish Cup Final Song)

22 May 2021, Hampden Park
Scottish Cup Final: St Johnstone 1, Hibernian 0
Clark; Rooney (Brown), Kerr, Gordon, McCart, Booth; Bryson (Davidson), McCann; Middleton (O'Halloran), Kane, Wotherspoon. Goal: Rooney 32.

'Immortality beckons', so said the banner outside McDiarmid Park, as Saints prepared for the Scottish Cup Final showdown with Hibs. The impossible dream was on. A chance to become legends, the lockdown legends. Blue and white was draped from rooftops, windows and door frames across Perth city. Flags, banners, colour . . . and anticipation. A new cup final song, an anthem to unite.

The Cherrybank Inn revelled in it all, the spot to stop for a selfie at their Saints wall, while even the giant grouse statue at the Broxden Roundabout was draped in blue and white – just as the Perth Bridge was lit up too. Amid the sadness of no fans once more for the season's showpiece, Perthshire displayed its support for arguably the biggest game in the club's history – a double was at stake.

Of course, there had been hope for supporters. In May, the Scottish FA applied to the Scottish Government to have 2,000 inside Hampden, only for an attendance of 600 to be granted. Just days before the final, a spike in Covid-19 cases caused the doors to slam shut again. At least the Covid issues no longer beset the Saints. Davidson could finally rest easy, just like his players.

David Wotherspoon

It was horrendous at the time. The boys had been working so hard all season and some were missing the semi-final. You felt so bad for them, so sorry, you just couldn't do anything for them. On the other hand, you are thinking about yourself and the rest of the team, you just had to be so vigilant and wary, stick strictly to the protocols. If you picked it up towards the end of that week after the semi-final, you could miss the cup final. It was a massive time for us, still chasing fifth place. It was a huge time to get those outbreaks, it was a horrible situation. With the boys missing the semi-final, it sort of pushed us and gave us that bit of fight to go on and win it for those not involved. The week after the semi-final I didn't do anything, but kept worrying I was picking it up. Just a little thing, like maybe if my nose was running or if I coughed once, it was like 'oh no, oh no'. The panic was there, the nervousness was there. You just didn't want to be one of those players. It was just a nerve-wracking time and I can't imagine how the gaffer and his staff were dealing with it going into that week. It was difficult, as boys were having to isolate for 10 days, so it was a worry about their fitness and everything. But, luckily, everything worked out and I hope he managed to get the team out on the pitch that he wanted.

Callum Davidson

I had no confidence from the Wednesday what team I could pick for the final. I just didn't know. It wasn't ideal preparation. At the back of my mind, I would have been so annoyed if we had lost the game because of Covid. Having to deal with losing so many players, that would have really hurt me. Day to day we were getting test results. I was nervous looking at my phone. I was getting text messages saying 'I was negative', but if I got a phone call I was like 'here we go'.

For the semi-final, we drove in cars on our own, because we had issues with the bus and a big coach. For the final, we had a couple of buses, as we didn't have any games after it and everyone was clear. The bubble was back.

Michael O'Halloran

It must have been hard for the others to watch on in the semi-final, but we were glad to get there, and I remember there were a few cases after that – you're worried. That's why I think a lot of credit goes to them, as a few had only trained one day, two days before and played in the final. The gaffer, as well, he kept calm, we trained and he kept us all focused. It must have been hard for him; he must have been pulling his hair out. That's credit to him and the staff, because it was handled really well.

Murray Davidson

I was washing my hands 20 times a day. I pretty much locked myself away for 10 days leading up to the match. I wasn't wanting to see anyone after what had happened before the Betfred Final. I was even missing out on meeting my wee girl because she was still at school. I just didn't want to take any risks. If I had missed the Hibs game and a third final, I would have been thinking 'I must be jinxed'. When I got the all-clear after the Thursday virus test, I remember thinking 'just don't get injured in the final training session'. It made looking back on missing the 2014 cup final and the Betfred that bit easier to take. I was so happy to be part of it.

Bobby Zlamal

No one knew what would happen. The club asked me to be ready just in case. Of course, the goalkeepers were okay but it was very nice of the club to invite me to the final because I wasn't part of the team. The players and coaches were very kind and supportive to me.

Paul Mathers

We invited Bobby to the cup final and he enjoyed it. He came back to the ground with us afterwards and I think he got an insight into what a unique club it is.

Willie Ormond's side were superb, going all the way to the 1969 League Cup Final and thriving in Europe. But there was no trophy. Alex Totten, Paul Sturrock, Sandy Clark, Owen Coyle and Derek McInnes all had their moments in cup competitions too, before Tommy Wright delivered. Now Davidson could lift two in his first season in management. Remarkable.

Stevie May

We were comfortable going to Hampden. We'd had the good times in the dressing room, and you get those memories, going back for the second time round. Whereas Hibs, for example, had lost two semi-finals, losing the Hearts one earlier in the year. You just think, 'we must be going in here with a better mindset than what they are, going into somewhere where they've had bad memories months prior'.

Zander Clark

I was in Ibiza (for the final in 2014). I was on loan at the time at Queen of the South. I hadn't played any part in it with Saints and we had had a successful season with Queens. The Chairman said he would take us away for a week, but I still made time to go and watch the final in a bar! We were underdogs going into this final, but we had played Hibs four times in the build-up and we had a good record. The boys had also stepped up at Easter Road in the league and we managed to get that job done. We were quietly confident we had a good chance of going on and making history.

Alex Cleland

We had a similar core to the team that won in 2014, with the likes of (Steven) Anderson, (Dave) Mackay, (Brian) Easton, (Frazer) Wright, (Chris) Millar, such good pros who managed to maintain their standards over the years. The new boys that came in have just looked up to those senior guys. They have adapted so well and it's just kept going like that. It's been brilliant to see.

Alistair Stevenson

I was here initially for 10 years, from 1993 to 2003. I moved to Hibs until 2012 and came back to St Johnstone, which I was more than happy to be doing. Over the course of the years there have been a lot of players that have made progress and come through. The first time I was here I had Danny Griffin, Keigan Parker, Kieran McAnespie and many more. They all broke through into the first team. Since I came back, it was a case of starting at the bottom again and building it up, and we're seeing that next generation starting to come through.

Ali McCann

I joined the academy in 2014 and we all got tickets as a youth academy member to watch the cup final at Parkhead. Spoony,

Mikey, Muzz and Mayso were all in the team that season and to do it again with them has been amazing.

Liam Craig
The good thing for us was that we had played the Betfred Cup Final under the exact same circumstances, in terms of media and everything that was going to happen. We could draw on that and know how the week was going to sort of go, and what to expect in that cup final week. In 2014, we were all away together the week of the final. This time, we couldn't even have a coffee together in that week. The pleasing thing for the final was everyone was there, nobody had missed out.

Glenn Middleton
We knew we weren't there just to make up the numbers. We had already won a Hampden final so that experience definitely helped the lads. We had made the top six and we also had a good record against Hibs. There was probably more pressure on us in the semi-final against St Mirren after beating Rangers. I'd say the expectation before the final was more from Hibs' fans. After all, the thinking of most people was 'why should St Johnstone be winning two cups in a season?'

There were shades of the final with Dundee United in 2014, such was Saints' record against Hibs. The Perth outfit had won their last three games against Jack Ross's talented, attack-minded side, who had finished third in the league. Indeed, of the last seven games between the teams, Saints had only lost twice. With his squad back intact, Davidson brought in Bryson to midfield, with Middleton earning his chance to start.

David Wotherspoon
Bryso had come in and played his part. He didn't start that many

games over the year, but he started the cup final against Hibs and put in a terrific performance. He always performed well. He is, again, one of the fittest boys I know, for his age. I think he is one of the fittest in the team. You really feel his influence when he is on the pitch, he always wants to get on the ball and is always trying to help others out.

Craig Bryson

I was obviously a bit gutted not to play a part in the Betfred Cup Final. Luckily for me, the gaffer near enough kept the same team from the semi-final for the Scottish Cup Final.

Liam Craig

As devastated as I was, I was buzzing for Bryso, who didn't play in the Betfred Cup Final. I knew Craig was devastated, because he'd never played in a cup final. I get to see Craig every day, and how he works, how he trains, how he looks after himself. Honestly, the way he goes about it, the way he is in the dressing room, the way he looks after boys like myself, Ali and Muzz is fantastic. He has a serious nature but still laughs and jokes: he is superb. I look at Craig Bryson in the same way I looked at Jody Morris and Simon Lappin – boys that have played at the top level, international, top of the Championship. You see the way they pass the ball, see the way they train, the demands they place on themselves, the way they tackle, the way they go about it. Fans don't see that day to day.

On the Friday ahead of training, Davidson gathered his squad at McDiarmid Park for a video session. Little did James Brown know there was some light relief to come at a nervous time . . .

James Brown

We sat down in the Muirton Suite, we were all in there, and

everyone's family was saying 'good luck', everyone's family had a message, family or friends. It looked more like a motivational video, showing everyone how proud they were. Everyone's family had done theirs, but mine hadn't appeared and I was still sitting there, thinking 'my family hasn't come up'. All were pretty serious messages, like 'so proud of you' etc. And then it came to the end, and I sort of recognised it was my parents' living room, and I thought, 'oh, no,' because, obviously you don't know my parents – they're so laid-back in life, in everything, they just take the mickey. Anyway, the message started off seriously, 'oh, good luck,' and they had 'James Brown, I Feel Good' and all that. Suddenly, the music came on in the background and they just started singing that song to me, obviously on camera! My mum and dad, they're pretty nuts, to be fair. It was quite nice, it was light-hearted, because we'd just had a barrage of quite emotional, serious messages, and they came on and just started taking the mickey. I just knew they'd do something to embarrass me. I went bright red, as well! It was nice to end it on that, but yeah, I knew, as soon as I found out the messages were coming in from everyone else's family, I just knew my parents would do something stupid – they couldn't resist! But no, it was funny: I quite enjoyed it. It did lighten the mood, all the boys and the staff loved it, so I guess it was nice to go out to training on a bit more of a joyful note.

In terms of the team, it must have been one of the hardest team selections for the gaffer, because we obviously had the Covid outbreak just before. We had boys that had come in and got two results, so you could have chosen probably anyone. There were probably about four or five positions, especially in the attacking positions, and even wing-backs, to decide on. Obviously, there were probably a couple of disappointed lads, as there will always be, especially final-wise. But when it gets to that point, when you're in the final, that goes out the window – everyone's there for the team. It was incredible really.

Craig Conway

I was a victim of squad rotation, I suppose. I was absolutely gutted not to play. Everyone wants to play in these games. You look at the League Cup Final and there were lads who missed out but played in the Scottish Cup Final.

Callum Davidson

Going back to the Betfred Cup semi-final with Hibs, I think we knew we were a good team. In the big games we had played up to that point, we played really well. It was, for me, more trying to curb their enthusiasm and excitement. It wasn't about motivating them to get them up for it, it was more how to make sure they stayed calm and focused and had the composure to go and play. We all knew what pressure there was to win, but it was a great pressure. It wasn't a relegation pressure. It was trying to make sure we performed on the day and to give ourselves the opportunity to win the game. To be honest, again I thought we did that. I thought we were superb.

9 mins *'Kane slices it over the bar!' (BBC)*

Liam Craig

I said after 10 minutes to El 'if we score first, we win this game'. Hibs had only beaten us once this season. If you look at Booth, he was comfortable playing against (Martin) Boyle. The back three were comfortable playing against their front two. I just felt we were the team that started well. It's very hard if you don't start well to raise your game to an intensity that you want to play at. I think our shape dictated that, even when we didn't have the ball.

Glenn Middleton

We controlled that game. That shouldn't be overlooked. We were confident from minute one. I know it was scrappy at times, but we believed we were going to win it.

27 mins 'Oh it's broken for Irvine!' (BBC)

Hibs almost led when the ball fell kindly to Jackson Irvine, but the Australian midfielder's low drive was brilliantly blocked by Clark.

Paul Mathers

Zander has shown he can handle the big occasion. He has been to Hampden and conceded one goal, making some big saves too. He is a lot more consistent now, doesn't make glaring mistakes and he has shown a great temperament. You don't get many bigger games than the Scottish Cup Final. He has made big saves at important times, maybe only one or two in a game.

Cue the 32nd-minute man. What odds for that to happen again?

32 mins 'Here's Wotherspoon, sold Gogic the dummy, in comes the ball and there is the goal. It is St Johnstone legend Shaun Rooney.' (BBC)

Shaun Rooney

To be fair, 'Mac' always shouts at us to get to the back post. I always get forward. If you don't go forward he starts moaning at you, and you don't want Macca on you, as well as the skipper. That's two people you don't want moaning at you.

I've always liked to go forward, but when you're tired, 'Mac's' always the one moaning at you, so it does make you get on the back post. The game against Celtic when I scored the header too, Macca was shouting at me from the side, 'get on the back post, get on the back post!' Obviously, it does help when someone's shouting at you – you always run up that extra yard.

Rooney became only the fifth player this century to score in both cup finals, joining Henrik Larsson, Barry Ferguson, Tom Rogic and Kris Boyd in that feat. It was the key breakthrough – and rich reward for the determined double tackle by Booth, who simply didn't give up. When the ball fell to Wotherspoon deep on the left, the ex-Hibee turned Alex Gogic with that customary 'chop' and sent a sweet, in-swinging cross to the back post, where Rooney's jump beat Josh Doig to power his header back across Matt Macey.

Callum Booth

I'm not on social media, so I've not seen anything about my 'tackles' name! But I certainly know that the Sunday we went out after the final and stuff, quite a lot of fans were talking about those tackles. I was obviously delighted to play my part in the goal, even if I'm probably not known so much for tackling! I'll take it. It was just two big lunges, really, two big slide-tackles. And then 'D', he had that bit of skill, put a great ball in and big Rooney's head got on the end of it.

Alistair Stevenson

I think the tackling side is something that Callum (Davidson) has instilled in Callum (Booth), obviously being a full-back himself. Booth was initially a sort of winger, more of an attacking player, and he is very good going forward. His defensive side wasn't as good but being a wing-back is ideal as it is a little bit of both. I think Callum has improved the defensive side of him. He has made some timely tackles, great interceptions, but he still has the energy and ability to get up the park and put in good crosses. He is on a high and he loves it. I know he just feels that he is appreciated here. He is well-admired and has become, in many ways, a fans' favourite, probably after the double tackle!

Three things now seem certain in life: death, taxes and falling for the David Wotherspoon chop. It now holds iconic status.

David Wotherspoon

I'm aware of it! I've been more aware of it this last year. But, it's funny, as it's been there for years. A lot of my team-mates and fellow players have always mentioned the so-called 'Spoony Chop' in training, or in games. It's always been mentioned, but I think it's now becoming renowned just because of that cup final clip! It's amazing to get that recognition of a skill. It feels great and it's tremendous just to be noticed for that.

When I go to cross a ball, it's not very often that I look up and have a look to see who is in the box. I try to put it in an area. But because I did the chop and had time, I actually looked up and just saw Shaun at the back post. I knew if I put it in the right area for him he would get his head on it. Luckily, I put in the right ball for him.

Chris Kane

Over time, you do learn where the midfielders are going to go, where they make their runs and play their passes. The only one that you're not too sure on is Spoony, because he does about 30 chops before he takes it up and then puts it in! But, obviously, Spoony's brilliant as well!

Liam Craig

I think David's ability is incredible. That's never, ever been in doubt, and it's just that consistency, 'can he do it week in, week out?' But I think this last year, the two positions that he's played in, wide-left of the three or that one just in front of the second midfielder on the left, he's picking up areas and pockets where he's hurting teams. He's comfortable that he's got that chop, but now he's actually producing more and more consistency in terms of assists, and probably still wants to add more goals. Look at what he's doing internationally – now he's away with Canada and trying to qualify for the World Cup in Qatar next year.

Alistair Stevenson

Spoony has been fantastic. He used to come in and train as an 11-year-old at St Johnstone. He would come in every Saturday morning. He got the chance to go to Celtic, then I was fortunate to get him into Hibs. I had a few there from Perth and would drive them up and down the road each day. I knew David was St Johnstone-daft. He played for Hibs at full-back, midfield, up front, got shifted around a wee bit and I don't think that helped him. This last season, in his preferred position, he has been absolutely outstanding. Now playing for Canada, who have such fantastic players, that has been great for him too.

Callum Davidson

David has been a big part of all three major trophies. He started all three games, with Mayso and Michael two of the three players to be involved, too. I had a system in mind when I came here and imagined Spoony playing probably in the two midfielders, but he is that clever and intelligent, and having watched a lot of games back, him playing on the left in a front three, he is the one player who gets it. He understands everything. That last season people say it's probably one of his best seasons. It's all credit to David and he is a Perth boy as well, growing up there. It's a great story and I'm delighted for him to be part of it all.

Saints led 1-0, and the minutes ticked on.

Shaun Rooney

My celebration was actually quite chilled, I can't truthfully tell you why. To be fair, you never think you've got the win until you are over the line and there was a long way to go.

37 mins 'It's Newell, he goes himself! And it flies over the bar!' (BBC)

Michael O'Halloran

I was on the bench and as soon as we got the goal, I felt confident. The back five have been terrific – I know who's been in there has chopped and changed a few times – and they are young as well, but they showed a maturity. I don't think Hibs had too many chances, and that's all credit to the way we defended. I thought it was terrific.

Bryson made way for Davidson midway through the second half, a major moment for Murray after his previous final heartaches.

Callum Davidson

It was a tough call between Muzz and Liam, but just the way the game was going it was probably suited to Muzz just to see it out. I'm delighted for him, the fact he contributed and played well. It showed how much of a squad we are.

Liam Craig

Muzz coming on, after missing out on two cup finals, was huge.

Murray Davidson

It all happened so quickly. I don't usually like wearing my shin pads as a sub, but I was all geared up and ready to go on if I got the call from the gaffer. I had everything on and I was good to go from the first minute. Liam (Craig) and a couple of others were out warming-up with me when I got the call.

Just as I was going on I remember 'Bod' our sports scientist (Alex Headrick) shouting that someone had lost a stud. I looked down and realised one of mine had fallen out of the sole. I am quite paranoid about them because I like to have a long stud on my boots, but I just had to get out there. I'd never have known if he hadn't alerted me to it. I just had to hope I didn't slip or make a mistake. That was all I could think of for the first few minutes out on the pitch. It's never easy to go on and get up to the pace of a game right away, never mind in a cup final.

74 mins *'Big chance potentially to win the cup! He goes down! St Johnstone penalty!'* (BBC)

Liam Craig

The only time in the cup final for me that I thought we might have a wee charge from Hibs was when we missed the penalty, but it never came. We pressed so well from the front, to the back. Kano is brilliant at it and Glenn was only here a few months and got it right away, showing it in the final.

75 mins *'It is Middleton, good save Macey! Kane's there! It's a double save'* .(BBC)

Glenn Middleton

It was a special day, even though I had that penalty saved which would have made it more comfortable. We had chances to extend our lead, we didn't settle for 1-0.

I had practised penalties the day before and I was confident stepping up to take it. But I think the keeper deserves credit for making a very good save. The game was still going on so there was no time to dwell on it. You can't mope around.

Brown entered the fray for Rooney on 79 minutes, aiming to keep Saints solid at the back.

Callum Davidson

(Jamie) Murphy came on towards the end of the game and caused a few problems. I brought James on and it was probably the only time I went really mad. He wasn't ready with his shin pads and I was going a bit nuts. But, again, I thought defensively it probably just helped us, at that period when we just needed to see the game out.

James Brown

My primary thought when I came on was, 'you're 1-0 up, just keep it that way, do whatever you've got to do to try and keep us ahead, just come on, be solid'. But yeah, I was under the cosh. You know when you're 1-0 up in the final, 15 minutes to go, you're going to get shelled. The ball's going to come in, they're probably going to have one big chance or something like that. I think you've just got to mentally brace yourself for that, you sort of prepare yourself for what's coming.

Liam Craig

The character we showed after Glenn missed the penalty – because that was an opportunity for Hibs – was excellent. One thing you do hear when there are no supporters is the encouragement that comes from the rest of the players. I remember warming up in the cup final with Mayso, and we were at Bryso or Ali or Kano to keep working. That's the sort of mentality this squad has.

Callum Davidson

I watched all the games the previous season and Ali used to run all over, had great energy levels. This year, playing with Liam in a two, he has managed to add a bit of discipline and understanding. I think international football has probably helped him to see how he can get better. He is an intelligent boy, he understands the game. He obviously had Covid before the final and in the last 10-15 minutes, I was like 'Ali, would you stop running?!' He was one of the players breaking forward, if you watch the game back. After the game, he said to me 'gaffer, I couldn't breathe after 30 minutes'. A little bit like Liam against Livingston. For me, Ali has been tremendous all season, and can play in a couple of different roles. I think he has understood the system we try to play. I still think there are things he can get better at.

Murray Davidson

If the penalty had gone in, I'm sure we would have won comfortably. The last five or 10 minutes of that final were the longest of my whole career.

Glenn Middleton

The belief in the team shone through again in the way we defended for the closing minutes. We rose to the challenge. That comes from consistent hard work on the training pitch. It all came together defending our lead to win a cup final. That is why you put in all those hard sessions on the training pitch.

O'Halloran replaced Middleton with eight minutes left, preparing to join Wotherspoon and May as cup winners once more after the trio also lifted the Scottish Cup in 2014 and the Betfred League Cup in 2021.

90+5 mins 'And that's it! A superb season has just become an extraordinary season for St Johnstone Football Club! It is St Johnstone's cup, it is St Johnstone's season. St Johnstone, League Cup winners 2021. St Johnstone, Scottish Cup winners 2021. Double winners. History makers.' (Liam McLeod, BBC)

Callum Davidson

At the end, it was more a sense of relief after what we had gone through in the weeks before.

'St Johnstone have done the cup double. Wherever you are, wherever you are listening, remember this moment. This is history. This is absolutely and utterly sensational. I'm trying to pinch myself to see if this is actually a dream or not. The players are slumped to their knees, I'm slumped to my knees.' (Steven Watt, SaintsTV)

Murray Davidson

What a feeling when the final whistle went. The celebrations made up for the finals I had missed. I have had loads of highs, and lows, in my years with the club. Playing for Scotland was another special moment for me. We finished top six again, which, on its own would have been a great achievement. But nothing comes close to the feeling of being part of the team that won the Scottish Cup that day at Hampden. It was on a different level entirely.

Glenn Middleton

It was incredible at the final whistle. I was very emotional. It meant so much from a personal point of view. In previous loans at Hibs and Bradford I had played under five different managers. That was an unbelievable situation. It's probably unheard of. But you can't afford to feel sorry for yourself in football. When things weren't going as well as I'd have liked I knew I had to persevere and keep believing in myself. This was payback I suppose. It all fell into place.

James Brown

The biggest thing is the relief, as soon as that full-time whistle goes, more than anything. It's funny, you don't actually probably enjoy playing in that situation, whilst you're there. But the relief afterwards is unmatched. You come on at 1-0, you don't want to be the person that comes off going into extra time or after you have conceded. It was a crazy experience, there's not many people that will experience that. That's just the pinnacle of anyone's career, let alone just one year, especially for a club like this.

Michael O'Halloran

Winning a trophy isn't about one game or the final, it's about the whole competition, the build-up, the getting there, each round. I think if you look at our squad, we all played a part in some capacity to get there at the end. We all wanted to play in the final, but for me, it's not all about that. I think you see that some boys played one final and some in the other. As a team, it was some achievement, and as I say, it's more than one game that wins you cups.

Spoony, the Perth High School lad, the boyhood fan who had been to Saints games since he was five years old, was simply in bits after his man-of-the-match display. 'I just want to say one last thing to my family back at home, watching, my kids, my wife, my mum and dad – thank you,' he said, the emotion pouring out of him, in the live post-match interview.

David Wotherspoon

I was in tears. After the League Cup Final, I was in tears then too, but I obviously didn't show it as much. When I came off the pitch, folk were congratulating me and saying 'well done' but I couldn't even speak to them. I knew if I spoke I would break down in tears. I was asked to go and do an interview and I was like 'I don't know if I can'. I got over to the interview, and they said 'just two minutes'. They asked me a question and I was like 'I don't know if I can speak'. I just couldn't hold it together, wasn't composed. I was struggling the whole interview to keep it together. It was just the relief and how much you work your whole life, basically, to get these moments. To create what we did for the club and that team, to create what we did over that year, the level of success we had, it just started to creep into my mind. This is what you work for, what you dream of, what you want in your career, and it's finally happened. I mean that day still hasn't sunk in, how good a feeling it was and how well we did last year. It just all came out in that interview.

In a previous interview earlier in the season, I didn't mention my wife and kids so I was determined to remember that and get it in. At the end, I knew as soon as I started saying it, I knew I was going to break down, and I just did. I just couldn't hold it in. My wife, Sophie, with the kids, sacrifices so much for my career. She does so much for me, it's great to, hopefully, make her and my kids proud in these moments. They are what I work for, they are what I live for. It certainly was an emotional time. It's been a boyhood dream, obviously from when I grew up watching St Johnstone as a kid, and my heroes like Nick Dasovic, Miguel Simao and Nathan Lowndes. I remember just watching that team play football, thinking where I wanted to be. Then to be doing it for that club, enjoying the success we've had with that club, you just couldn't write it, really. I'm sure the boys who are from Perth agree. It's just an incredible feeling to be doing what a fan would want to be doing. It's just an amazing feeling and something I'll never forget. I've obviously got three medals, so one for each kid, Mia, Alina and Brady. I've also never been beaten playing at Hampden in six games. It's great to compete there as a player.

Throughout the squad and coaching staff, it was time for fond reflection. The club had emerged unscathed from no fewer than 13 cup ties across a colossal campaign.

Callum Booth
I suppose when I left Hibs, I never really thought I'd ever win the Scottish Cup. When you're a wee boy, it probably does sound

clichéd, but you dream of scoring a goal to win the Scottish Cup, and the furthest I'd ever been before was the quarter-finals. I'd never have thought I would have the chance to win the cup. It was unbelievable.

Glenn Middleton

Everyone who knew me was happy for me, my friends and family. They knew it had been uphill for me at times. It was an unbelievable squad to be part of. I'll always be grateful to the lads for the welcome they gave me.

Alex Cleland

I won the double at Rangers as a player. I knew what it was like to win two trophies. It's so, so hard. To come and win at St Johnstone, now as a coach, it's something special for me. Nobody would expect St Johnstone ever to win the double. To be part of that coaching journey and turn around to say when it is all finished 'well, I was part of the St Johnstone management team in the season that we won the double' is special. When you get ex-players phoning you up and texting you, just saying 'Alex, that's remarkable for St Johnstone, the management team and the staff' it's nice. That's from players that you respect, that have won trophies. There were many names, but the text from Richard Gough was so special. For him to take the time to say 'Alex, what an achievement for you, Callum, Steven, the club and the staff to win a double' I thought that said a lot for Richard, who has won so many trophies and is a legend in the game. He knows how special it is and how hard it is, so that meant a lot to me. To win any double is just remarkable. When your fellow players and coaches, those you have worked with in the past and have the utmost respect for, just send you a nice little message, it was great for me.

Jamie McCart

Initially in the season, we just didn't get that wee bit of luck. I think after January it kind of clicked for us, and we went on our run. I'm considerably young in terms of football, I'm only 24, so Liam Craig was saying, you know, 'don't expect to get to a cup final every year'. I think for boys like Liam, Craig Bryson, you know, they're 34, they'd gone their full career without winning a major trophy. Then they won two and I think it shows how much it meant to them. Even now, I think it's probably not fully sunk in for a lot of us.

Michael O'Halloran

I think I've been lucky to play in two really good teams to win trophies, looking back to 2014 and now. The first team I came into was great. The one thing I've always noticed is that in the dressing room the lads have always been brilliant. There is a bit of contrast between the teams as well. If you look at the team when we first did it, it was an older, experienced team, whereas now, it's a much younger team. Even when we won the first one in 2021, it gave us that belief and the hunger to go and do it again. I think maybe winning the League Cup helped, as we'd got that bit of experience of going to Hampden and playing. If you look at the two finals, I think they were two really mature performances.

Bryson, having scored a goal for part-time Clyde to knock Celtic out of the Scottish Cup on Roy Keane's debut in 2006, had another cup memory to treasure – and silverware to show for it.

Craig Bryson

I managed to play a part in St Johnstone's history. From where I came from the previous two years, to go on and play in the semi-final and the final of the Scottish Cup, win the double and finish fifth was incredible. When you're growing up in Scotland, being Scottish, the Scottish Cup Final is always the showpiece game of the season, always the one you watched growing up. One day you think 'I would love to be a part of that'. The further on in your career you get, the more you think it's not going to happen anymore. To get the chance to start and win was honestly incredible. It was a great couple of weeks after it, it's just a shame we were in a pandemic and the fans, those who have been fans for life, couldn't be there. A lot of people have lost their lives, but from a selfish point of view we were just gutted that our families and fans couldn't be there to enjoy that special moment with us.

Alistair Stevenson
It was just a fantastic season. There were so many highlights. I was very proud of the double, as there were some boys that I helped get there, so to speak. There were also two I had helped at Hibs, Booth and Wotherspoon. Although David has always been a St Johnstone supporter, he came down to Hibs with me. It was great to see the two of them feature. I was also filled with pride too when I got a text message to say Ali had been picked for Northern Ireland for his first full international. I remember getting back home to try and record it. He also played against Italy in a World Cup qualifier, against Marco Verratti, and that was a great moment for me. Plucking Jason Kerr from boys' club football and managing to get Liam Gordon to St Johnstone from Hearts were great moments too. To see them all coming through, along with the ones that have been there for a longer journey like Chris Kane, Zander Clark and Stevie May, that was just fantastic.

All the players had attributes growing up, but they've all had different journeys, going out on loan, coming back, some getting a breakthrough a wee bit quicker than others. It was fantastic to see and meant so much to everybody. I just kept thinking 'I bet you guys never thought you would still be all together and winning cups?' It was a great thing to see their pride in what they had achieved. We have provided players of the standard to go on loan and I think now, after the season we've had, it will be easier again for players to go on loan. They realise it may be a better option to go on loan and get experience, rather than playing for the Under-19s or other youth teams. A lot of the current first-team players have played a number of games on loan.

Jason Kerr

I've known 'Gordy' for a while, and we've both been out on loans. I always say this now, after the cup successes, we'd never have thought when we were playing together in the Under-20s that we'd be going and doing this.

Liam Gordon

No, we were cleaning the boots of Ando and 'Fraz' (Frazer Wright).

Jason Kerr

They won the Scottish Cup in 2014, and you're thinking 'they've done something so special'. You'd never think, obviously when me and 'Gordy' were washing their boots, we were going to go and do it as well.

Liam Gordon

We actually said recently when we were walking out to training, and there's the big picture of Ando celebrating his goal in the cup final in 2014, it is mad. Coming out of that changing room as an Under-20 player, you always used to think, 'I wonder if we'll ever be on this wall, scoring a goal or whatever'. Now you've got the photos of us down there with the trophies and all that, it's surreal, it really is. It's amazing.

Craig Conway

If you don't get on the pitch you can't help but feel you haven't really played a part, even if you had a role in getting there. Any footballer will have that niggling feeling but it is a squad game nowadays. The manager made the substitutions that he felt were right and we won the cup. I had won the cup with (Dundee) United and I feel sorry that Saints missed out on the normal experience with the fans. The players had their celebrations, of course, and certainly made the most of it. But a lot of these lads might never win another cup and for them to be denied the full experience was a shame.

Ali McCann

Having been at the final in 2014, I would never have thought I would be in a double-winning team. It's been outrageous. It was a little weird, to be fair, without fans, especially in the first few league games, but we were well used to it by the end. It does feel different, it can be hard to get yourself up for it, but eventually we got used to it and when we hit form it was fine. But the games at Hampden were weird because you just think 'of all the seasons to win the double, it is the one with no fans'. It was a bit annoying, but they were still great days and I'm sure all the fans enjoyed it from afar, from wherever they watched it.

Callum Davidson

For me, it probably hasn't sunk in quite yet, what we actually achieved. To do the cup double, wow! Aberdeen did it, a team of full internationalists, and that's it, apart from Rangers and Celtic, in the history of Scottish football. We are the only other team to do it. Hopefully, it gives every other small club the opportunity to believe they can go and achieve something special.

It will be remembered, but whether it sinks in or not, hopefully we can remember it with the fans and celebrate as we should. I think reaching the top six was still an unbelievable achievement to get there as well. For me, all credit to the players and the staff. I'm leading the ship so to speak, but they are the ones who go on the pitch and do it every week for me. Ali, for example, is a young lad and has achieved a cup double at the age of 21. Liam did it at 34, I never did it as a player. Ali has got to remember that, enjoy it, and try and use it as springboard to have an amazing career, because he has the potential to do so.

I really have got to thank everyone, from me as the manager, for how they worked. I can't say in one game I thought their attitude or energy levels were poor. We lost two bad goals in the space of two minutes at Livingston, but apart from that I can't remember a game where I went 'oh no, I'm worried about the players'. I genuinely can't. For me to say that is testament to the group of boys and what they did over the season. It's a big thanks to them. They were incredible.

The impossible dream realised. Perth St Johnstone, double cup winners. The greatest season in the club's history. Don't you ever, ever forget it.

NINE

HEAVEN AND PERTH

'Forget the rest, St Johnstone have achieved the greatest single-season success Scottish football has ever known.'
Eric Nicolson, The Courier

Salute the Hampden heroes! If there was a sense of utter disbelief at it all, perhaps an individual who had witnessed the season at close quarters could instead put the pictures into words . . .

Rory Hamilton, Commentator
As a commentator, football fans continually try to second guess where your allegiances lie. It should be irrelevant and shouldn't be detectable. My job is to put words to the pictures and to try to capture the feelings of those to whom it means most. All that I want to emerge are stories – events that are unpredictable, that shock and stir the emotions.

Last season, St Johnstone provided exactly that. I've asked many people if it is the greatest achievement in domestic Scottish football history – and I've yet to receive a comparable rival. To win the Betfred League Cup for the first time in the club's history was enough of an achievement. I thought I'd used up all that I could say about St Johnstone on 28 February, only to have to come up with even more, come May.

From Zander Clark's heroics at Ibrox, to Shaun Rooney's back-post leaps, I allowed myself to become wrapped up in the history they were creating. For Callum Davidson to mastermind it in his rookie season as a manager just makes it all the more incredible. For those two events at Hampden Park to occur simply shouldn't be possible in modern football. But it happened. For Saints' fans, it was the impossible dream, and as the story was forged, it was a joy to tell.

In becoming the first non-Old Firm team since Aberdeen in 1989-90 to lift both cups, it was quite extraordinary. The Dons then operated far closer than now in financial terms to Celtic and Rangers, the other two sides to have done the double. For Saints to become the fourth was mind-blowing. A small Perthshire club under the tactical nous of an astute manager – remember, replacing a club legend – had turned around a slow start to the season to do, well, the unthinkable, in the midst of a global pandemic. Fact or fiction?!

Callum Davidson
To be honest, I said in *Our Day in May* it was probably one of my greatest achievements being part of the 2014 Scottish Cup success, but I think it's slightly been surpassed. I don't think it will be repeated for me. I hope it will be for St Johnstone, hopefully we can go on to continued success in Europe and more. But, for me, I think it is probably the highlight of my career. It might get done again, but I think we are the first to do it in the respect of a smaller, provincial club. To me, this eclipses anything I've done in my career. Winning at Wembley as a Scotland player was probably the highlight of my playing career (in 1999). As a coach and manager, this will be very hard to surpass, without a shadow of a doubt.

Guy Melamed

It was incredible for the gaffer, winning two cups. It was like Zinedine Zidane winning the Champions League in his first season as manager of Real Madrid.

David Wotherspoon

I'm not sure it will happen again. Not just for St Johnstone, but for any team outside Rangers and Celtic. You look at it and think 'how is that going to happen to anyone?' It's such a massive deal. During the season, it felt like we were going from week to week, just carrying on. I think having that run of games non-stop helped us. It certainly helped me, personally, just to carry on playing. Having that game after game kept us focused and driving towards what we wanted.

Zander Clark

I still have to pinch myself at what we achieved. I still get goosebumps talking about what we did. When my time as a player does come to an end, it will be a time I look back on with great memories.

Murray Davidson

No one in their wildest dreams would have thought St Johnstone could win two cups in one season. Every year after signing for the club our priority has been staying in the top league and we have done that comfortably.

It was no different when the gaffer took over, despite all the top-six finishes and qualifying for Europe when Tommy was in charge. The success of the club has been built-up over a long time and every manager and player has played their part.

Like so many others, I am proud of being part of the most successful time in the history of St Johnstone. I'll look back in years to come and only then realise how big an achievement it has been. It's something no one can ever take away from you.

Alex Cleland

Fans may look back one day and say 'did that actually happen? Did we have the season we had?' They will always look back and say 'wow,' as it was unbelievable. It has felt surreal at times. I just look back on my years at St Johnstone and how it has all developed. If anybody had said to me 'you will be part of Callum's coaching team in his first season and win the double,' you would be like 'no, you are away with the fairies!'

Danny McNamara

I was called back to Millwall after Christmas so I was really jealous of the lads when they went on to win two cups. Maybe I was the toxic one holding them back. They didn't look back after they got rid of the dead wood! But I got first-team football back at Millwall and ended up with the Young Player of the Year Award. That was down to my time at St Johnstone and I'll always be grateful to the club. I watched every St Johnstone game I could after I went back south.

James Brown

I sent Danny a text, winding him up. Obviously, he's gone back to Millwall and done well but deep down, it would be burning him a little bit.

Jamie McCart

It's still not sunk in. I think if you had asked anyone when myself and Shaun signed, we'd have never predicted what was going to happen. I mean, when we finished fifth and had the League Cup, everyone was like, 'incredible season' and then to obviously go and finish it with a Scottish Cup win – I think the best word is 'fairy tale'.

The 'will it ever sink in?' comment is a common theme. It's no wonder. Was St Johnstone's double a bigger achievement than Leicester's English Premier League title triumph in 2016?

Michael O'Halloran
They were saying the odds were 10,000-1? And what were Leicester to win? 5,000-1? It's incredible, isn't it?

Elliott Parish
It kind of puts it in its own perspective a little when you think what an achievement it was for Leicester, and then a further few thousand for Saints. 10,000-1 and it came off? Quite incredible. When Leicester won the league, there were £10 bet stories but I've not seen one person put a quid on St Johnstone to win the double. That again sums it up!

Shaun Rooney
I certainly wish I'd had a bet on for the 10,000-1 for St Johnstone to win the two cup finals!

You would have got some odds, too, on the Saints' boss doing a Klinsmann-style slide across a beer/champagne-soaked Hampden floor!

Liam Craig
The best part about it was when Mayso put it on Twitter on the bus. I was sitting just behind and saw it, and I was like 'uh, oh, I don't know if the gaffer is going to be happy about this!'

Callum Davidson
I think I got more comments about my slide than winning the double! I got a lot of texts to thank me, but the slide got attention! Shaun Rooney did a slide and kind of got three or four

yards and I thought 'that is a pitiful effort'. Macca went 'c'mon gaffer, you can do it!' I said, 'Macca, the only thing I'm worried about is if I land and I stick.' So Macca got a couple of cans of beer and starts squirting them on the floor. I took my top off and thought 'stuff it, I'm doing it'. To be fair, I was quite impressed with the slide myself. The problem was, as I was sliding, this door came into view. I'm thinking 'it's going to slide open', as it was swing doors and they were open all game. I hit it and I went 'oh my goodness, that was sore!' I got up and I could see some of the players not quite sure. I just went 'yessss!' And everyone went 'yessss!' and went nuts.

It's had 1.3 million views – that was my daughter, Eilidh, telling me! It's a great part of the story, isn't it? People will probably remember the slide, just as much as the trophy wins. I didn't fine Stevie, because he cut it early before my big belly was walking back! I was delighted with him. I actually gave him a £50 tip! I was delighted he did it.

Guy Melamed

Everyone was celebrating in the dressing room after beating Hibs. The gaffer's slide across the floor is the funniest moment I had in Scotland, by far. I will never forget it. It was right in front of me and I saw him hit the wall. It was a different side of the gaffer we saw, but he deserved to celebrate. He is the most successful manager in St Johnstone's history. If he couldn't do it then, when could he? He is such a good manager. He helped keep me positive in the early days when I wasn't starting games. I have seen some coaches get very angry and lose it completely, but he was always very calm when the results weren't good in the beginning. He was patient and it finally worked out for him and the team.

Davidson, in his first season in charge, was now on the same stellar list as, among others, Jock Stein, John Greig, Sir Alex Ferguson, Walter Smith, Dick Advocaat, Martin O'Neill and Brendan Rodgers in lifting both the Scottish Cup and League Cup in the same season.

Callum Davidson

It's a great list to be on. It probably won't sink in. It's like when I was a player, I didn't really remember what I did as a player until I had finished. As a manager, it will probably be the same. I'll always look back and go 'oh that was pretty good, and I was part of that'. Some people chase money. I've never been a money chaser. When you have finished playing, it's about what you have achieved. You remember those times. I will remember the dressing room for ages, the win at Ibrox, the bus going home. Just things like that, they just live in the memory with you. Even back at the stadium, these things just live with you. Like the 2014 Scottish Cup, going down the High Street will live with me forever. It's something I'm delighted to be a part of. St Johnstone is a big part of my life and I'm just delighted I'm part of the success story.

Among the players, many could understand how Davidson's will to win –which many have also seen first-hand on a golf course – had paid off.

James Brown

Obviously, budget-wise, we're nowhere near some of the other teams, but the gaffer just lets us go and do what we're best at, to go and express ourselves. The boys love that and I think that's how he's got the best out of the players.

Paul Mathers

You got a feeling at some point this could be something really special. In a strange season with Covid, everyone spoke about bubbles, but Callum, Alex, Macca and myself were probably in a football bubble. We didn't realise how much of a bubble we were in until we came out of it. It was pretty relentless at times, but it was really enjoyable. We were in a mindset of feeling, I hate to say it, unbeatable at times. I think for any team to lose only four games from January to May is great.

Scott Tanser

I had the best four seasons of my footballing career with St Johnstone and didn't regret coming to Perth, especially having two cup medals to show for it. It's just a shame I didn't get a chance to say goodbye to the supporters. Tommy and Callum helped develop my game hugely, and Callum being a left-back himself in his playing days definitely helped me.

Jason Kerr

He would have been forgiven for having a dodgy first season, it was his first ever season as a manager! But the amount of hard work he puts into everything, never mind just football, is incredible. He's good at golf, good at tennis, he's good at everything! I think he's just a born winner, to be honest.

It's been a great year working with him, and I think I speak for the rest of the players when I say everyone's enjoyed it. Everyone's coming in every day, enjoying training, wanting to work hard and to perform. There's a good group of players who are honest with each other and with the manager's philosophy. We've obviously got ability, but to have the work rate that we do as well, it's only going to breed success.

Liam Gordon

In leaving Hearts, as soon as St Johnstone came calling I got the opportunity to move back home, playing for the club that I supported, who my friends and family all support. I didn't look at it as a step back. There are bigger clubs in Scotland, but none of them have the heart and the soul of this club –that's why I love playing for it. Everyone will constantly write us off and we keep proving them wrong, and I think that's what spurs the guys on as well. I was on loan from Hearts at Arbroath and that's when Callum and Alex came and watched me. For me, I was only moving forwards, and it's paid off.

Beyond the manager, there were stories for folklore across the season. Rooney, the rampaging wing-back, with the beard, the power, the passion and the personality. A cult hero.

Shaun Rooney

You've got to enjoy everything. How often will things come around? I won the FA Trophy at York, and League One at Dunfermline, but this has been another level. I don't know how many trophies I'm going to win in my career, I don't know what's going to happen. I could break my leg tomorrow or something like that, and that could end my career – you've got to enjoy every moment you can. My social media accounts went a bit crazy, to be fair, but I don't really bother. It probably is worse for me, getting more famous, more people knowing me!

Fans talk about the No. 32 shirt, but no I'll keep 19 – that was my ma's birthday, I'll just always keep it. That's the first number that's been good to me and it took a while to find it! She passed away, she had cancer. It was the second anniversary on 19 July so that's what that is.

I'd like to go and get some more trophies, hopefully with St Johnstone. You always want to go and win other things. Life goes on, 100%. Every day, you've got to find yourself a living in the world, just go and enjoy yourself. If anything happens, it happens. I will always have a smile on my face.

Then there were Melamed's key strikes...

Guy Melamed

Supporters were very kind to me on social media and I saw that some were calling me the 'King of Israel'. There was a 'Guy' banner for me at the stadium as well. It is strange to have played for a season and never had the chance to play and celebrate goals with the fans. It is the dream of every player to run to the crowd when they score a goal.

The players told me how good it is to play in front of 50,000 and 60,000 fans at Rangers and Celtic, as well as in front of our own supporters. Maybe one day I will come back to Scotland. Looking back, it was a great decision to come to St Johnstone. I was out of my comfort zone but I will always be happy for that.

It was fantastic to win two cup medals and it is something I will tell my children about one day. I had lost a cup final in Israel and that was traumatic. The celebrations after the finals were amazing for me, seeing everyone singing and drinking beer and champagne. I had learnt all the famous St Johnstone songs by then. It was special to enjoy it in another country, another culture. There was a lot of interest in the finals from Israel. The reporters all knew about Celtic and all the cups and leagues they had won but now my team had won two trophies.

. . . and Wotherspoon becoming the only St Johnstone player to start and win three cup finals . . .

David Wotherspoon

The celebrations were special, they will always be remembered, and I'm so proud to have achieved that feat.

. . . yet with a nod to his fellow experienced midfield colleagues.

If you look at their ages (Bryson, Craig and Conway), people might think they don't have the legs anymore. But all three played their part and proved everyone wrong. It was just a great balance and I think the manager worked that well, using the players when he needed them, giving them a rest too. It shows with our success.

Craig Bryson

When I signed for St Johnstone, without sounding disrespectful, I'd never have imagined that we would win two trophies. If you had said to me we were going to win the Betfred Cup and the Scottish Cup in the same year, I probably would have thought you were mad! For a club like St Johnstone to go and win the double in the gaffer's first year of management is absolutely incredible.

I've had some good times in my career, like down south at Derby, scoring a hat-trick against Nottingham Forest, which is like the equivalent of an Old Firm game up here, and getting promoted to the Premiership with Cardiff. It's a wee bit hard to compare, but when you are winning two trophies for St Johnstone that's got to rank definitely in the top three of my career. In the end, a top-five finish and two trophies, I don't think you can ask for much more, to be honest.

Craig Conway

There were still all the restrictions in place and we couldn't enjoy it to the max with the fans. But the history books say that St Johnstone won both cups in one season so that can't be taken away from them. They will look back on it all with fond memories.

Personally speaking, I'm not really one for history going into games. I think that can affect your performance if you get too carried away with it. The belief instilled by winning the League

Cup definitely played a part. That experience a few months before certainly helped us.

Liam Craig

It's huge credit to the staff and players as we could have easily downed tools after the League Cup Final. But to go and get the top six, finish fifth and guarantee Europe the week before the cup final, then win the Scottish Cup Final, dealing with everything we had to do, was just remarkable.

To have played over 400 games for the club as well is just incredible, and to do it during a period of success for the club over the last 12 years has been even better. I don't really know when it'll sink in, if it ever does sink in. You definitely appreciate it more at 34, and emotionally it hit me massively.

David Wotherspoon

Ando used to remind Liam every day (of missing two cup wins). It was just a bit of banter but I'm sure it hurt. I'm sure he can look back now and be like 'it doesn't matter'. He has got two cup medals now, played a massive part in them. We had the disappointment back in 2014 with Murray, Tam Scobbie and Tim Clancy missing out on the final. For people like Murray to now come back, have the heartbreak of the League Cup and then go and win the Scottish Cup, it's a massive thing. For Liam and Murray, who are a huge part of the club, it was great to see them get that reward and success.

And what of Kerr lifting two trophies as captain at the age of 24?

Callum Davidson

Jason got the captaincy role and I think he's grown in it. He's got a really good assistant behind him in Liam who can pass on experience and give him good advice, as he's a young captain.

Liam has worked really hard with him, talked to him all the time. Jason is a great character, wants to work hard and just wants to win games of football. We probably missed him in that little period over Christmas, I think results showed that. Since he came back, I think he has given himself every opportunity to try and push into the Scotland squad. He will be remembered as the double cup-winning captain and that's something you can never take away from Jason.

Jason Kerr

I just kept the armband and I got to lift the trophies! I would never have thought that, after getting the captaincy, I would go on and lift two trophies, two seasons later. It's just absolutely ridiculous to think, but I'm just so buzzing that we did it.

You probably would have thought after 2014, 'we'll take that, we've won a major trophy, that's fine, we don't need to win it again for another, what, 20, 30 years'. To go on and win the double, especially with the money that's at Celtic and Rangers, and obviously you've got Hibs, Hearts and Aberdeen with good squads, you feel like the league's not designed for us to go and win the double. But the team, from the turn of the year, we turned in a lot of good performances, and a lot of clean sheets as well. Some days I still pinch myself.

Or of McCann pushing the team on at the age of 21?

Ali McCann

It's been a brilliant start to my career. It's surpassed my expectations. I've only been in the first team for two years and for last season to unfold how it did was special. I got my head down, worked hard and hopefully my team-mates appreciated the work I was doing. I tried to put in a consistently high level of performance. We had a sticky start, bedding in a new system, but from Christmas onwards everyone was brilliant and we got the rewards from that. Personally, I just felt I did my job. I was a 'steady Eddie'. The only thing I probably lacked was scoring more goals and I would like to get myself into more positions to do that.

And of O'Halloran and May, now also with three medals from 2014 and 2021?

Michael O'Halloran

It's been mad. It's somewhere I've always felt comfortable. It's always been, for me, where I've played my best football. To come back to the club and win the double, I probably never dreamt it. Sitting here, having won three cups, it's a bit surreal! It's a great group.

Stevie May

I suppose it doesn't really even feel real when you think, 'can I grasp what's actually happened?' It was when I saw the two cups together, I thought 'this is a big, big achievement'. When you see them individually, you kind of forget about the other one. Then when we went back to the stadium after the Scottish Cup and got to celebrate with both the cups, it was special. It's just a shame the fans couldn't be there to see it, but they know the magnitude of it after going so long without winning a major trophy. For three to come along in the space of seven years, it's kind of incredible.

I've only really played three seasons, I think, well over 150 games for Saints, so I'm averaging a medal every 50. We'll see how the next 50 go!

We've all contributed in different ways. I mean, if you look back on games maybe we should have scored more, but it's not the be-all and end-all at times, as it showed. A lot of 1-0 wins, while we had games where we had loads of shots and crosses and it wasn't happening, but we stuck to the plan and the way of playing, and we reaped the benefits come the end of the season. It's a special team.

Back in that 2013-14 season, it was kind of like everything was about goals for me and everything I was hitting was going in, but that last season we've not had someone who's hit 20 goals or scored every week – it shows you don't always need that. If you've got a good group of boys who are willing to work hard for each other and do both sides of the game, then you don't need to have a striker or a midfielder who's doing absolutely everything. Everyone can chip in and you can have a foundation, defending well as a group. There are many ways to win trophies and be successful.

I always knew I wanted to play football, but I was never thinking of what trophies I was going to win or anything like that. It was getting to the next stage, getting full-time. That's the one, when you were at school, 'I want to be full-time, I want to do this', and then it's kind of getting there and then next, 'I want to break into playing first-team football'. I never played for a season or two, then I went out on loan, and it's a case of one step at a time. I had a taste of success, obviously when I was on loan at 17 we won the league at Alloa, so that was a big thing, getting that winning feeling, and you can never get enough of it.

When we won the first one in 2014, it was like, 'this can't get any better', and obviously, I left the season after. I went to England and then to Aberdeen and you're thinking 'what more can I achieve?' Then I come back and we lift two trophies! It's just kind of crazy. Obviously, it helped with Rangers going out in 2014, but this time we managed to put Rangers out ourselves, so it made it that bit sweeter. And the way we did it, it was a special time.

It's been a pretty hectic year. Obviously, you've got this horrible pandemic, and then at the same time, winning the double, and my son, Axel, was born. This year will stick in the memory for a number of reasons! It's been a special time, at the same time as all the bad stuff going on in the world.

Steven MacLean

We've done well, obviously, but it's trying to move on and get better all the time. You look at the nucleus of the team and they can still all improve. Go through them all. Look at the improvement in Chris Kane, for example, and I can see Stevie May kicking on again and getting better. Collectively, we want to keep improving.

Mayso's work rate for the team has been unbelievable. Hopefully he can get back on the goal trail. He still scored vital goals for us last season, did really well and played a lot of games. He is a top player. The numbers he got in that 2013-14 season were incredible (27 goals) and it will probably be hard to repeat that, but there is definitely a 15-goal striker there. Hopefully he can kick on.

Alex Cleland

We've had a lot of new, good players come in, like Rooney, McNamara and McCart and the emergence of McCann, and Bryson with a bit of experience. But I think the players who've been here for a long time have got to take a lot of credit. Zander Clark has been here a while, Stevie May has been away and come back, as has Michael O'Halloran, then you have mainstays like David Wotherspoon, Liam Craig and Murray Davidson. The team has maintained standards over many, many years. Those players who have been here seven, eight, nine, 10 years and are still here, are a massive part of the success St Johnstone have had. Among players we have lost and players we have added, these boys deserve immense credit for keeping their standards up. The standard that I've seen in training having been involved a long time, from that group of six players, is brilliant. Through different managers, we've been able to keep that main core of players. That is one of the secrets of our success, keeping players that know our standards, in training and games, and know how to marshal dressing rooms. New players that come in get to know what is required straight away and that is all credit to the group of players who have been here so long.

After the Hampden celebrations, subdued once more without fans, a Perth party back at the club at least allowed the players to finally relax. The team bus was welcomed back by some jubilant fans, and the players bounced and sang along with supporters behind a ring of steel erected round the stadium due to Covid.

Michael O'Halloran

Obviously, that's the only thing that we missed – the fans. I remember the atmosphere when we played at Celtic Park in 2014, it was incredible. When we got to go through the city the next day on the open top bus, and then the parade, that was something that lives long with me. Even when we came back here to the stadium after beating Hibs, and you saw some of them coming out, I just felt that wee bit for them that they couldn't do what we did in 2014.

James Brown

The weirdest thing about it was the celebrating, but there was no one to share it with. Even on FaceTime with your family: they're not there. That was probably, in a way, the saddest part about it, I think. But obviously you can't knock the achievement.

Craig Bryson

After the Betfred Cup, I think I was back in my house about 6.30pm. I was thinking 'we've just won a trophy and I'm sitting in my living room!' The lads did say if we did win the Scottish Cup we're going to have to try and do something, within Covid guidelines. We managed to get out for a few drinks and enjoy it. It made it sink in a wee bit more, having that celebration.

Bobby Zlamal

It was a good feeling to celebrate with the players after winning the Scottish Cup. The squad had made me very welcome and I had a couple of beers back at the stadium in Perth. I was driving to Edinburgh the next day so I couldn't celebrate as much as I'd have liked on the Saturday night! I was drinking water, which was a pity.

They even asked me to have something to eat at the (Cherrybank Inn) pub in Perth the next day. I didn't expect that, but I wanted to say goodbye and wish them well for next season. It was quite emotional for me. I could see they were a good group and I think that is why they won the double. They totally deserved it. Football isn't just about good players. The x-factor is important and the squad, gaffer, coaches and even the kitman were very strong together.

Alex Cleland

Both cup final celebrations were pretty quiet, compared to other parties that I've been part of after winning leagues and cups before as a player! And compared to the last one we won in 2014! It was a pretty quiet affair, but it was still memorable. We celebrated as much as we could in the circumstances, as we deserved it.

Jamie McCart

We couldn't celebrate after the Betfred win, especially as that was peak lockdown. Everyone went back to their house, pretty much. But for the Scottish Cup, I think we enjoyed that. I remember getting back to the stadium and it was good, obviously, to have some fans there. I know it wasn't ideal with the restrictions and what was permitted, but it was good to see some and at least we had a wee bit of a celebration.

David Wotherspoon

It was fantastic. It went pretty much all night at the stadium. You didn't want it to end. Having just been in a cup final, you were absolutely exhausted at the same time. But you just carried on, you had to live it up as it's not going to happen very often. It was just tremendous to have everyone together. To finally be able to celebrate a wee bit, even in a closed environment, with everyone, was brilliant. It is something we all shared together. It was a shame that families couldn't come and join in, but these things happen and we still managed to celebrate and enjoy it as much as we could.

Liam Craig

Aye, it was horrible, not having supporters there. But I'd rather win two cups and finish fifth with no supporters than get relegated with supporters! It's been a tough year or so for everybody, but to give our supporters what we did, you just can't make it up. I know how the club works, I know the supporters, and I get on great with them, every relationship I've got is brilliant. But it's only brilliant because I come in every day with the right attitude and give 100% hard work for the club.

Steven MacLean

For the fans not to experience what the players and everyone did at the club, you were so disappointed for them. I remember it from 2014, with families being there too. It has been devastating for the fans and the players as a whole. You are just gutted for everybody.

The party was changed days! I did have a good few beers, but Callum and I left early and we let the boys get on with it. I think some of the players and the Chairman stayed quite late, but we left them at quite an early stage. On the Sunday, we went up and had some breakfast and met the boys for an hour and let them kick on again! Yeah, changed days when you are a coach!

At McDiarmid, together as players, coaches and staff, they could all look back on critical moments in the season. Winning away at Dundee for the first time ever in the Scottish Cup, big Zander getting his head on Craig's corner to spark bedlam at Ibrox for a first Scottish Cup win over Rangers, Middleton's exquisite free-kick at Hampden. The list goes on . . .

Chris Kane

Everybody talks about the 1-1 draw at Hamilton when Guy scored quite late on – that was a massive point. There were loads of games in the season you think you should win, but the point does help. Overall, this past season is going to be hard to beat. It's one that we'll never forget. It was massive.

It's the most I've played in a season, 40 games in total. I do feel like it probably is the fittest I've been. But obviously, I've worked on my upper body as well, so I'm not getting shoved off the ball as easily. I've been here going on 11 years now, since I was 15, so personally, it was my best season. It is a bit of a blur, but we can look back on it and hopefully try and replicate it by winning trophies.

James Brown

The spirit and togetherness here is fantastic, because it's a smaller group – that can sometimes get lost at a bigger club with more finances and greater numbers of people and players. When Hayden (Muller) was coming up (from Millwall on loan), he rang me and asked me about the club. The first thing I said was, 'There are no egos, there's no arrogance'. You see it even with top sides like Manchester City and Liverpool. Even though they're all big-time players, the manager ensures they're still just as happy as the players that don't play as much and doesn't let anyone get carried away. I think it's something that's massively overlooked in football, but we have that in abundance.

Elliott Parish

People say all the time 'what an achievement it is'. It is still quite surreal, when you think about being just the fourth team to ever do it. It was a huge collective effort. I only played one game in each of the tournaments (Kelty Hearts in the Betfred Cup and Clyde in the Scottish Cup) but it was so pleasing to be involved. For the club to go and win the double under the circumstances we faced is crazy. You will probably get your head round it more when you finish football and start watching it from a neutral perspective and see what other clubs have achieved. I will probably be looking back in 30 years and nobody will have done it again! You look at Leicester winning the Premiership, I know it's maybe not quite on that level, but St Johnstone winning a domestic cup double really is incredible. It was a heck of a few months.

It's my first two medals in football. I've been everywhere, down in England, every division, up here, and never come close. I think the previous best I reached was the fifth round of the FA Cup, not even coming close, and then you go and win two in a year! Look at Liam Craig. What a great career the guy has had, still going strong now, playing at a fantastic level, and finally won two cup medals. It's testament to players like that, and how rare it actually is. Ali McCann is going about with two medals thinking 'that's only my second full season!'

Callum Hendry

I think scoring the equaliser in the last-16 of the Betfred Cup suffices for a medal, hopefully! Everyone wrote us off last season, especially after the start of the season. Everyone thought, 'oh, Saints could be in a relegation battle'. But we've said that the last few seasons, and we've ended up in the top six, or top five. Since I've been here, we've had slow starts, then we tend to have a top-six surge. We just proved everyone wrong last season, it was amazing.

Jamie McCart

For me, the most important thing was consistency, to do well and keep my place in the team. I played nearly every game, was available for selection, and just kept trying to put in good performances. I was just happy to be involved in such a historic season.

Callum Booth

Momentum and confidence is big in football. When you're in the moment, you're just focusing on the next game, you know when you're doing well. But when you sit back now and you look back, it was just crazy what happened, the run that we went on. I still can't really believe it, how we got into the top six, winning all those games at Hampden, winning the double and finishing fifth. You actually need to say it out loud to believe it! Nothing really changed, it was just that we got a wee bit of luck, and that's what you sometimes need. From Christmas onwards, we were just superb.

For some at the stadium party, it was a rather late finish . . .

Liam Gordon

I'd love to be able to tell you what time Liam (Craig) and Zander left, but I don't even know what time I left myself!

Liam Craig

Walking out of the stadium at half-seven on the Sunday morning with big Zander shows that I certainly did enjoy it all! It just shows what a good night it had been. Zander and I were staying in the Holiday Inn, down at The Maltings, just off the roundabout towards Inverness. I said to Zander, 'We need to go up the road' – albeit there weren't many people left at this point. We were still in our tracksuits, I still had my strip on! Zander, I think, still had his strip on. This was still in the stadium at half-seven! So we walked out and I said, 'Forget a taxi, it's a five-minute walk, we'll be fine, five minutes'. He's got his bag, I've got my bag, still got the strips on, walking down into Perth from the stadium to the hotel, and people must have been going, 'look at those two, whatever, walking down there'.

I remember seeing flags out and thinking how funny it'd be, at half-seven in the morning, to just go and knock on someone's door and have me and Zander there, absolutely rubbered, with our strips on, just to see the look on a fan's face. Fortunately, we didn't! It might have actually been an even better story if we had! We got to the Holiday Inn, and I remember the boy behind the counter – people were all in having their breakfast – just saying, 'Good night?' we just looked at him and went to our beds.

I actually FaceTimed Laura walking down the road, and she was like, 'Where are you?' and I showed her Zander walking next to me. I said, 'We're just walking back to the hotel.' She said, 'You are drunk.' I said, 'No!' She was getting the kids out of bed. Then at 11 o'clock in the morning, me and Zander went down to the hotel bar, and a couple of the boys met us and we went into the town. I got picked up at eight o'clock on the Sunday night. We didn't see a lot of supporters, but it was brilliant.

Zander Clark

The birds were certainly up tweeting in the trees as me and Mr

Craig left the stadium. It was a good night followed by a good day. Folk were going for their morning rolls and papers and me and Liam were zigzagging our way down the streets of Perth. It was brilliant to be able to go and enjoy it properly. With two cups and a European spot, it's madness to think about. I think if you had said to anybody before the turn of the year that would be the outcome at the end of the season, you wouldn't have believed it.

Further accolades came. The club was awarded the historic Freedom of the City of Perth. Kerr was selected for the SPFL Premiership Team of the Year – and Davidson fired a new course record 62 at Dunblane New Golf Club! Then those memorable European nights with the giants of Galatasaray followed. Those Hibs-supporting Murray brothers might have put Dunblane on the sporting map, but Davidson is on their tail.

Callum Davidson
Andy and Jamie are big Hibs fans and I had a game of golf with Jamie at the golf club ahead of the final. It's great for a little town like Dunblane to have the attention.

Liam Craig
We all have brilliant stories, brilliant memories. Hopefully the club can build on it, hopefully it gives the club a bigger support now, and people really want to buy into what the club's about. It hasn't just been about this year, it's a number of years. Obviously getting the Freedom of the City is just another great achievement for the club, and rightly deserved for the way it's been run. I'm not sure what it means, to be fair, but certainly, I'll look into that and take full advantage of it!

Steven MacLean
I don't really look back. I said that when I still played. I'm hungry

for success. I think once you've experienced success you want more. I'm just driven, I want to do well. Yeah, we've achieved a heck of a lot, but I kind of want to keep going, keep getting better and try to achieve as much I can with the club and with Callum. You just want to keep trying, to keep getting better and to move forward.

Do I want to be a manager one day? Probably. But I'm in no rush whatsoever. I'm just enjoying what I'm doing, learning all the time from Callum. I've got a heck of a lot to learn, but I love my role, love working with Callum, Alex and Paul and everybody at the club. The Chairman and the board have been excellent with me, as a player and as a coach. It's a credit to them for allowing me to come back, as well as Callum. It's a big thanks to everyone at the club for bringing me back.

Michael O'Halloran

Looking at it now, some people will say, 'Where do you go from here having won the double?' But for me, being part of this group, it gives you that hunger to go and get as high up the league again as possible and try and win trophies again. I feel the management want to go and build on it, which is great. For me, it's been an incredible time playing for St Johnstone. Looking back on this, I couldn't have imagined it. It's all about the standards that we've set here now over the last decade or so. I'm looking at our team now and I'm thinking, 'you know what, it's a right good squad. Why not go and build on this?'

Liam Gordon

It's crazy. It's not sunk in, and I'm not sure if it ever will. Doing wee things such as this book interview, you think about it more, and you kind of realise the effect and impact you've had on the people of Perth. I look forward to going back to my school, Perth High, and actually show what's doable and what you can achieve if you just put your mind to it. I go back to my time at school, and by no means was I the best player, but I just had the best head on my shoulders. I just try and instil that into some of the next generation that are coming through Perth now. It would be amazing, not just for me, but for all the boys to go round and show off the trophies to the local school kids – it would be a lovely touch.

Steven MacLean
Listen, some days I wake up and go 'how can we have just won a double at St Johnstone?' I do shake my head sometimes!

Don't we all, but it really wasn't a dream, it wasn't fiction. Childhood dreams were realised through the telling of a fairy tale footballing season. A story for the ages. For so many, 2020-21 was a time to forget, but not in the wonderful history of St Johnstone Football Club. Please, make mine a double.

GEOFF BROWN, OWNER

It was back in 1986 when I took ownership of Saints. The club were struggling, it was dark days. Fast forward to 2020-21 and we all endured dark times, living through a global pandemic. Yet, what positive light the club provided, what joy they have given to the fans. From a football perspective, it's something that I don't think any St Johnstone supporter ever dreamt could happen. From a life perspective, I think it's certainly one of the best things I've ever been part of. I thought 2014 was special, but the last season was simply remarkable. We had 11 Scottish-born boys on the park – for both finals – and that is unusual, a credit to them all.

It's 10 years now since I passed the Chairman role on to Steve. I've obviously got assets in the business (GS Brown Construction) and assets with St Johnstone, and he's managing director of the building company and also the Chairman of the football club. He works incredibly hard, is a busy man and he's obviously a son I'm very proud of. He's won three trophies after all! We had a few tears in our eyes after the final wins at Hampden and shared feelings together just like any father and son.

Going back to the summer of 2020, it was fairly clear in Steve's mind that Callum should be the man to take over. When

Tommy left, the side wasn't broken. It wasn't something that you had to sort of restructure or whatever, it was just a case of keeping going what had been there. Callum initially, it has to be said, between August and December, faced questions that were asked. 'Is this guy just a good coach or is he a manager?' And the next six months of the year certainly proved he was a manager!

Looking back to the period up to Christmas, the system was there, but the problem was that we just weren't scoring goals. Providing we kept playing well, it was always going to change. The first thing any side does is try and close the door at the back and that was what Callum endeavoured to do. Danny McNamara did exceptionally well on loan from Millwall, but Callum also had Shaun Rooney on the books and Rooney's a character. All of a sudden, Rooney came in and gave him a wee bit of extra firepower.

Throughout the season it was a strange time to watch football given the Covid-19 situation. It was obviously great to be at home games, but you miss the fans, of course you do. I picked the away games to go to. For obvious reasons, I didn't go up to Dingwall, for example. There were two or three away games I didn't go to, given the Covid challenges, and I just watched them on TV. There's really not much pleasure sitting in an empty arena, and it's bloody cold, just for the sake of it. You could be sitting way back in the stand and hear the players shouting to one another. It's really eerie, but it was about who could adapt. You look on and you say, 'Can you thrive, can you perform?' We certainly did.

Various games, away from the finals, stick in my head. Melamed's goal against Hamilton. Oh, that was tremendous. Zander at Ibrox. That certainly was a moment! Then there was Kilmarnock away, the 3-2 comeback win.

We weren't at that game at Killie, nobody was really there for St Johnstone as Covid was bad at that point. We gathered at

McDiarmid and had SaintsTV on and we watched the game from there. We were 2-0 down, how on earth! They had no right to be 2-0 up and we were getting sucked into a relegation battle at that point. The second half, wow! That was the death knell for Kilmarnock.

Then there was the Hibs game down at Easter Road, and we scored early on through Middleton. I was so comfortable sitting in my seat, sitting on a 1-0 lead.

They just felt so secure. It wasn't a case of 'Are they going to be able to put some pressure on?' The pressure never came. It was the same with the 1-0 game up at Perth, a Liam Craig goal, and Hibs huffed and puffed, but they weren't able to get through. I think the overall thing for me was the competence of the back three playing together across the season. That, in actual fact, broke the hearts of the opposition and allowed them to play.

Also, I think over January, Covid quietened the market quite a bit. Thinking back to the past, if we got to December, January, you could have been losing some players. This time we got a chance to keep them together. I'm not sure there were really any transfers as such.

Winning the League Cup, something the club had never done, against Livingston in February was obviously special. It was strange, sitting in individual seats, rows apart, and shuffling out of the stadium without much celebration. Of course, we were keen on a drink and there was nothing in the stadium and there was none on the bus either! It was quite comical, actually.

I was coming away and Roddy (Grant) says, 'We're going to have to go to an off licence.' I said, 'Roddy, an off licence?' 'Aye,' he says. 'We can't go back dry!' So, we diverted the bus, and we went and finished up in front of Celtic Park.

We had to change buses, as it happened, as the bus that we were initially on, the driver's window had exploded during the game! So we get on another bus and Neil Docherty was driving, and Roddy says to Neil, 'Neil, we're needing drink,' and Neil says, 'We'll just go along and see what we can find.' So we're heading back home, out of Glasgow, and up comes a turn off, for Cumbernauld. So we turn into Cumbernauld, and I said, 'There's a Tesco Metro, that will do. Oh, and there's an Asda, that will do.'

So, Roddy and I jump out of the bus at Asda and we've got our suits on, all dressed up, and we went in, and the people there knew that we'd won the cup, so we were going along with the trolley, chatting to folk and putting in beer, beer, more beer, and then back to the bus.

Of course, we go back to the ground, and there's 200 or 300 people at the ground and it was a bit crazy. The police made us stay on the bus, before we could get into the club lounge. But we had left the drink on the bus, so out we went again to retrieve it! The Perth-based players came back and it was just into the lounge and a few drinks there, it wasn't exactly going daft.

After the Scottish Cup win against Hibs, I came down the road from McDiarmid, chatting with my brother in the taxi, and I got home about quarter to 10. I fell asleep on the chair. I woke up in complete darkness at two o'clock in the morning! All these days, drinking is not exactly my strong point.

You have to celebrate these occasions, of course you do. After all, I think we have to remember who we are. We are St Johnstone: we are a team that's playing out of a city with a population of no more than 50,000 people. You've got an area which gives you a catchment of something like 120,000 people. When you compare that to like St Mirren, for example, the town's 77,000 people. You compare that to Inverness too, their population has really boomed.

And to stay where we are is really difficult, it's hard. I take great pride in our loyalty to managers, going all the way back to Owen Coyle's arrival in 2005 really. Look at the success we've had since then, through Derek (McInnes), Steve (Lomas) and Tommy.

This time last year we could never have been thinking about this happening. It's a time to savour, to take great pride in. There are only four clubs that have achieved the cup double previously, and the three other clubs all had massive budgets and national players. Look at what our St Johnstone have achieved! After my 35 years' involvement with the club, it really is wonderful. To all Saints fans near and far, raise a glass and enjoy it. It may never happen again.

THE MATCH REPORTS

BETFRED LEAGUE CUP FINAL
Hampden Park, 28 February 2021
LIVINGSTON 0 ST JOHNSTONE 1
By Matthew Gallagher, Perthshire Advertiser

Legends. Forever legends. St Johnstone are the 2021 Scottish League Cup champions. The trophy proudly in the Perth cabinet for the first time in its history.

This was a nerve-wracking 90 minutes at the national stadium. It was always going to be. But Shaun Rooney's first-half header sent this little club from the Fair City into dreamland. History was created.

Manager Callum Davidson, in his first season, will never be forgotten. He didn't care how this game of football was won. That Rooney header was more than enough and smiles on faces at the full-time whistle were delightful to witness.

For the supporters, required to watch from home, this would still be a momentous day. They would be dancing and singing. They would be in tears.

Pre-match nerves would be completely understandable. The same would apply for those tasked with taking to the field.

Davidson made only one change from last week's comfortable victory at Fir Park. Craig Conway, who played a starring role in the semi-final, was given the nod while Guy Melamed dropped to the bench.

Midfielder Murray Davidson hadn't recovered in time from a calf knock to be included and that was gutting news. He has been a fine servant and deserved his moment at Hampden. There was experience in the middle of the park in Liam Craig, though, who lined up alongside the talent and energy of Ali McCann.

Energy was on display in the third minute when Chris Kane set up a Perth counter attack. The ball was worked to Conway who waited and slipped it into the path of Rooney. He had made up great ground but his cut-back was blocked and rolled into the hands of Robby McCrorie.

Up the other end, Zander Clark was soon called into action. The Perth shot-stopper was at full stretch on 17 minutes to touch a Josh Mullin strike behind for a corner. What a save.

The opening half-hour had been a battle and one where Saints had struggled to get a foot on the ball. Numerous fouls and stoppages in play were certainly not helping the flow of the game. In many ways it was a similar opening as witnessed in the semi-final against Hibs. And then, as happened on that fine day, determination shone through.

With 32 minutes on the clock, Rooney wrestled in front of his man to nod Conway's corner into the bottom corner. He wheeled away in celebration, joined by jubilant mates. Those on the bench and sitting in the stand punched the air in delight.

His goal-scoring form has been incredible and as the half-time whistle approached, he wanted another. Despite being 35 yards from goal, he fancied his chances but this time McCrorie grasped the ball.

This squad was now 45 minutes away from legendary status. How they would love a strong start to the second half.

They certainly did begin on the front foot and when McCann's cutback found David Wotherspoon, it appeared the advantage was going to be doubled. He guided goalwards but McCrorie was positioned well to block and then Chris Kane was inches from turning in the rebound.

Perth boss Davidson would be delighted with how his men were fighting for the cause. They certainly looked more comfortable on the ball. Clark in the Saints net was being protected superbly well by captain Jason Kerr, local lad Liam Gordon and Jamie McCart. What a shift.

Livingston did begin to apply pressure as the game entered its latter stages. But this was Saints' day. And it will be one never forgotten.

SCOTTISH CUP FINAL
Hampden Park, 22 May 2021
ST JOHNSTONE 1 HIBERNIAN 0
By Matthew Gallagher, Perthshire Advertiser

The full-time whistle sounded. Players crashed to the floor in disbelief. High up in the Hampden stand, there were tears of joy from chairman Steve Brown and all associated with St Johnstone Football Club.

Manager Callum Davidson punched the air in celebration and would later slide topless across a champagne-soaked dressing room floor. Yes, you read that right.

Emotional supporters danced and danced and danced back in the proudest city in Scotland. Long into the night it would continue. Many a glass was being raised and everyone – absolutely everyone – was ordering doubles.

As captain Jason Kerr waded through gleeful team-mates to take centre-stage and lift the 2021 Scottish Cup, it still wasn't sinking in. It probably won't sink in this week, this month or even this year. What is certain is that this team will never be forgotten.

Winning the League Cup and Scottish Cup in the same season was tagged as the impossible dream. But when it comes to St Johnstone, nothing is impossible.

There was a banner hanging up the back of the East Stand in recent years which was adorned with the message: 'Underestimated Since 1884.' Nobody will be underestimating this group of players ever again. They are not just local legends. They are legends of Scottish football.

Standing in the way of an unthinkable cup double was Hibernian. A bigger squad, bigger budget, bigger fanbase and the rest of it. But certainly on Saturday it was the Perth club who had the biggest heart.

The opening minutes were nervy as expected. Substitutes and players not named in the squad were kicking every ball in the stand. Young striker John Robertson in particular was caught up in the occasion and was screaming for free-kicks at every opportunity.

Then there was legendary midfielder Liam Craig unable to remain in his seat. Up, down, up, down with every attack into Hibs territory. That's what makes this club special. Whether a kid yet to make his mark or the most experienced of operators, it means everything.

There is the never-say-die attitude and on the park that was more evident than ever with 32 minutes clocked on the giant electronic scoreboard.

Twice on the left flank full-back Callum Booth looked second favourite to win the ball. Twice he dug deep to retain possession. Man of the match David Wotherspoon was now in control and produced the cleanest of chops to feint back onto his right foot. *The Wotherspoon Chop.* It is a glorious piece of trickery witnessed on a weekly basis.

Hibs midfielder Alex Gogic had not been paying attention and was left completely bamboozled as the former Perth High student delivered towards the back post. What a delivery.

And there was Shaun Rooney. The bearded hero in blue who climbed high above defender Josh Doig to guide a beautiful header into the back of the net. His love affair with Hampden – he netted the winner in the League Cup final – continued.

Not long before the special opener, Saints goalkeeper Zander Clark had pulled off a smart save with his left leg to deny Australian international Jackson Irvine from close range. It was a vital stop.

You would have expected Hibs to come out all guns blazing in the second half. But there was a lack of fight. Saints wanted this more. Skipper Kerr, Liam Gordon and Jamie McCart were relentless in winning everything in the air and on the deck. The energy of Ali McCann and Craig Bryson in the middle of the park was key.

Bryson had run himself into the ground by the 64th minute and on came Murray Davidson for the moment he always wanted. He battled, scrapped and put his body on the line to keep the capital club at bay.

It was his pass in the 74th minute that deflected into the path of hard-working striker Chris Kane. When he was upended in the box by Paul McGinn, referee Nick Walsh wasted no time in pointing to the spot. What an opportunity it was.

Tasked with the responsibility from 12 yards was Glenn Middleton. His performance had been packed full of energy, drive and determination but his attempt was saved by Matt Macey. Hibs had a lifeline, yet they still did not look up to the challenge.

Like we have witnessed so often, Saints pulled together again. They defended remarkably well through to the last kick of the football. And when the full-time whistle arrived, players slumped on to the turf in amazement. There were tears. The Scottish Cup was theirs.

The trophy was lifted and the party kicked-off in the dressing room.

Many decided to take a moment to themselves on the field of play to call loved ones and simply attempt to digest what had just been achieved. Here's to you, St Johnstone Football Club – make ours a double.

FROM THE FANS

Eilidh Barbour
Broadcaster

'Never say never because limits, like fears, are often just illusions'
– *Michael Jordan*

Inspirational stuff from a man who didn't believe in defeat. But I think even the great Mr Jordan would've been hard pushed to come up with the achievements of a wee team from Perth over the last 12 months.

Being a St Johnstone fan is something that I was born into. My dad was a supporter, they were my home team growing up, they were part of my childhood, part of who I was and very much a part of who I am today. And while I wouldn't change it for the world, you don't support St Johnstone for annual trips to Hampden, European adventures or lifting trophies. That stuff doesn't happen. Or certainly, it didn't.

But for all the punching above our weight that has gone before in our recent history, no one could have predicted or imagined quite what the strangest of seasons would deliver. They called Leicester City winning the Premier League an impossible dream.

I'm not sure what comes after impossible, but the League Cup and Scottish Cup sitting side by side in a glass-fronted cabinet in Perth is it.

And to witness it all from behind a TV screen, in the living room of the house I grew up in, just adds to the utterly bonkers scenario. But as those trophies were lifted high in the air, caught on camera for all of us at home, there was nothing but heart-bursting joy and pride.

There aren't words, just emotions. Emotions that will live forever in each and every Saintee, to be dipped into from time to time for the rest of our lives.

Season 2020-21 will be remembered for many reasons. For us, it will never leave us. It really was a season like no other and for that, St Johnstone, I thank you.

Colin McCredie
Actor

In the summer of 2020, St Johnstone were at a crossroads. Our greatest ever manager, St Tommy Wright, had left to be replaced by his young protege Callum Davidson. The country was in the midst of a terrifying pandemic and the future of Scottish football looked grim.

I like to think that late one night at the crossroads of Crieff Road and Newhouse Road, Steve Brown came across the devil and was offered a deal. St Johnstone can win the cup double but not a single fan can be there.

As a fan who first visited Muirton Park in 1979, the thought of Saints ever winning a national cup was fanciful. The shock and joy of 2014 still felt fresh but none of us was to realise at the start of the year that winning cups would be like waiting for buses!

I was disappointed but resigned to the fact it was extremely unlikely I'd make a game all season. It was fine. Saints were ticking along and the live streams and radio coverage were OK. Little did any of us know what lay ahead.

As we gloriously progressed through first the League Cup and then the Scottish Cup, I actually started to enjoy not being there. The pressure was off. A nice routine of a pie in the oven for half time and a couple of beers and being able to watch on the big TV was a reassuring part of the second lockdown. I'm not going to lie – Saints' achievements made lockdown a lot more bearable.

It was one of the few joys and there were so many highs along the way. Big Zander, Ali's penalty and the 'Bellshill Cafu'. All witnessed at home with my family around me. It felt great. I did still hope I could pull off a 'Cosgrove'. Sneak inside Hampden for 'work' purposes but sadly only one chancer managed that . . . twice!!!

Never have I been so proud of my 'diddy' team and to be inundated with dozens of congratulatory messages from friends and family was an absolute tonic.

I still have to pinch myself about what actually happened and what our boys achieved but, without a doubt, 2021 was the best of times and the worst of times.

Stuart Cosgrove
Broadcaster

In Praise of David Wotherspoon

Foreword
In the days after St Johnstone beat Rangers to reach the Scottish Cup semi-finals, the BBC asked me to write a script in praise of

David Wotherspoon. It was made into a short film and broadcast just before cup final kick-off. This is what I wrote:

When young boys dream of playing football, they imagine they are David Wotherspoon. The weaving runs, the elegant feints, the effortless nutmegs, the audacious step-overs followed by a defence-piercing pass or an effortless bending shot. Spoony is football at its most romantic.

This is the history we were all taught to embrace – Davie Cooper, Andy Ritchie and even Dalglish – all those gods, sent down from heaven to play on grass.

David Wotherspoon is preparing to play in a third national cup final for his hometown team, the club he supported as a boy. He is Kieran Tierney without the megaphone, a superb footballer who has quietly got on with the game, cherished by those he grew up among.

St Johnstone fans place great faith in local boys. Liam Gordon, Stevie May and Spoony all feature in our cup final squad, and are fans on the pitch, hard-wired to the club, the town and its people.

Even on the annual replica shirt day, Spoony can be trusted to rake through the cupboard and join in with the fans.

So why has he not played for Scotland? Well, you may not know this but buried away in the arcane rule book of Scottish football is a requirement that St Johnstone players must never be picked for the full national team.

Although Spoony played international age group football as a teenager at Hibs, he has always been an outlier for the Scotland squad. Understandably, as the years progressed, he looked elsewhere and has now been capped by Canada, scoring his first international goal this year.

David Wotherspoon is why I watch football. Some say he should cut out the fancy stuff, others say he lacks killer pace. But

I go to watch football not athletics, leave that to Usain Bolt. Art is sublime, effort is every day.

A great passage of play can be as breathtaking as a goal. In our historic 2014 final against Dundee United, the sight of Spoony tormenting Andy Robertson will stay with me for life.

Watching St Johnstone's greatest season has been a mixed blessing – regret that fans were not there to witness it but balanced by the sheer audacity of the achievement.

My son is still learning what love is all about. When we beat Rangers in the quarter-finals, he emerged from the kitchen brandishing a huge wooden spoon. 'I still like Stevie May,' he pronounced in mischievous triumph. 'But not as much as Davie Spoon.'

Afterword

I only have one regret about the script. I was too nervous to imagine the audacious goal that would win us the cup, the one where without any assistance from NASA, David Wotherspoon sends the Hibs midfielder Alex Gogic into orbit before crossing for Shaun Rooney to head home the decisive winning goal. I have watched Spoony's cut-back on video-clips a thousand times and will never tire of its game-changing beauty.

Nick Dasovic
Former Midfielder, 1998 League Cup Runner-Up

From Afar in Canada

It's an amazing achievement what the football club has done, it truly is. Callum has done an incredible job. Tommy started to play some younger players, and Callum has taken that on. The real bravery is when you keep playing them, and credit to Callum for doing that. The players are mainly Scottish, while the number of youth academy graduates, six in total, who won the cups is incredible. It's extraordinary!

You don't get that anywhere in Europe, I don't care if you are Real Madrid or Barcelona. That, to me, is one of the biggest points of the season. That academy is producing players year in, year out now. That bodes well for the finances of the club, and perhaps eventually selling players on, if the time comes and the price is right. The next young player needs to come along into the team. The whole pipeline is kept flowing by Alistair Stevenson, he deserves a big, big pat on the back. He is an amazing gentleman too. I spent a lot of time with him when I was at St Johnstone. The job that he did when he was with us, the person he is, how calm he is, understanding youth players – he has been amazing for the club. It's incredible a young player like Jason Kerr has captained the team to two trophies at his age.

I pretty much logged on to see games when I could over the season. I was back in Scotland in December 2019 when Tommy's team lost 4-0 at Motherwell. When I started watching Callum's team, it wasn't just that they were young, they were playing some pretty good football. They defend with three, with the two wingbacks, and they are good. They are well-versed, know when to press, when to attack. They are a well-coached team and that is down to Callum and his staff, as well as the players taking it to heart.

Guy Melamed came in with a decent pedigree behind him. Saints were maybe struggling to score, but for Callum there was no panic. It was about bleeding him into the team, not starting him, bleeding him in. What happened? It came to fruition. There is a method to why Callum does things. I listen to a lot of interviews with Callum, watch a lot of football, and he just always has that same demeanour. I remember the Aberdeen game at Pittodrie, and when there was the penalty decision, but Callum said, 'it is what it is' and he just moves on. There is no real emotion from him in a good or bad away, so that shows me a young football manager who has grown up and understands the dynamics of football. He knows there is another day, another session, another game, he truly gets it.

For me, David Wotherspoon was the top player for the team. When I first saw David with St Johnstone he was a very good player. He is on a different level now. If he had come to Canada earlier, I think at his age just now he would have 50 caps under his belt, such is his quality. This Canada team is the strongest we've ever had and David deserves to be a starter from what I've seen. Alphonso Davies at Bayern Munich is now one of David's team-mates, while Jonathan David won the French League with Lille. These are top players David is playing with in the national team, but David has also helped put St Johnstone on the map again here in Canada.

St Johnstone is part of me, even from afar. It's nice for me to rekindle memories. The 1990s team didn't achieve what this group of young men did, but I think we brought the team back to a certain level of respect. I'll never forget the stadiums being full, playing in front of the fans and the League Cup Final of 1998. It was a different era for Scottish football, different money involved in the game and it was difficult to maintain any kind of success as it was hard against quality players. This group has just taken it to a completely different level and they deserve to be playing in front of packed houses again, showing off those trophies. It was a crazy year and it's testament to what the guys have done. Callum is automatically top of the club's pedestal for what he has achieved, but Tommy was the greatest manager before then. When he left, I'm sure he had no idea this was going to happen.

For the Hibs Cup Final, I saw the final song concept 'Down to the Wire' pop up on Twitter and thought it was brilliant. I started following the group and they asked if I could do them a favour. I was like 'absolutely'. I wanted to be part of it as it's an awesome time for the club. I was air guitaring, but the drums were real! I wanted to help in any way I could. St Johnstone gave me a home, which I will never forget.

When St Johnstone do things like this, it gives our group of the 1990s a chance to come back to life! For me, the memories are of being in a dressing room with Allan Preston, Roddy Grant and Alan Main, the list goes on, and the banter. Coming to work was a joy at McDiarmid Park. It was a beautiful stadium for us. It's nice to be remembered and associated with a club like St Johnstone. Maybe for my next visit I'll start practising on the bagpipes!

Jo Wilson
Sky Sports News Presenter

'St Johnstone have done the double' – words I never imagined I would get to say live on air as the full-time whistle blew on the Scottish Cup Final. It was certainly a far cry from my first ever game at McDiarmid Park in the 1990s – a match against Motherwell abandoned at half-time because of snow. The highs and lows of being a football fan!

Speaking of highs, I don't think any of us imagined in 2014 we'd be celebrating the pure elation of seeing our team win a Scottish Cup for the first time ever. THE FIRST TIME EVER! I will never forget not only the match, but the way the whole city of Perth got behind the team – I've never experienced anything quite like the atmosphere at the trophy parade the day after. It was also something I never thought I'd come close to experiencing again in my lifetime.

And, in a way, I was right, because last season there would be no fans celebrating in the stands, nor a trophy parade through the city. But what was amazing to see once again, was Perth lighting up in blue and white and people getting right behind the team, from their homes, in whatever way they could.

I watched the League Cup Final at home but was on air during the Scottish Cup Final this year, knowing at full-time I'd be revelling in delight or smiling through disappointment. And what a delight it was saying words I never dreamt I'd be saying. Not just that St Johnstone had won the cup but they had done the DOUBLE – and all in Callum Davidson's first season in charge. It was unbelievable. And quite the turnaround from match reports I had to do earlier on in the season!

Colleagues were congratulating me as I left the building and as I came back in the next day. It really did feel like a fairy tale story that had captured more than just the hearts of the fans, and in a year we all needed something to celebrate!

Eve Muirhead
Olympic Medal-Winning Curler

I have probably followed Saints more this last year than I have for a lot of years. When I was a little kid, I followed religiously all the time, saving the cuttings out of the papers and having them on my bedroom wall. Obviously, when you get a wee bit older, that kind of dies down a little. I think my following over the last year is because of the whole situation the country was in. There was very limited sport for myself, so I took an interest in whatever sport was going on. Saints were doing very well and it's always exciting watching your local team, especially managing to lift two trophies. It was pretty special.

The disappointing part was no fans, but I was lucky enough to be able to witness them winning the cup back in 2014. To be there and see that, you never actually thought that day would happen again. This last year, winning the two cups, I got so nervous watching sport. I get a lot more nervous watching sport than actually playing, which is quite weird. I think you feel like you have full control when you are taking part, but when you are watching you have zero control. I hate it – I get so, so nervous. It's horrible watching. I must say I was a nervous wreck for both finals, but it was all good fun. It's so great that the rest of the family are Saints fans and when you see the way Perth dealt with the victory, with the flags and scarves everywhere, it was a time we won't forget in a hurry. I grew up in Blair Atholl and it's been a great time again for Perthshire.

The moment that probably stands out for me is Zander's header at Rangers in the Scottish Cup quarter-finals. It's not often you see a goalie having an impact when it comes to a goal, do you? That is a memory that I can still picture. It doesn't happen often. To me, that was definitely the moment that kind of drove them to winning the Scottish Cup.

I know Callum quite well. I used to see him a lot at the University of Stirling where we used to train as well. To see him get that golf course record at Dunblane back in the summer was just incredible. He is one of those guys who is just good at everything!

As soon as things get back to normal, as such, let's hope that what St Johnstone have done has started something special for the fans. Let's hope we can get more young people involved in sport and get McDiarmid Park packed out, families taking along their kids to see this double cup-winning team. I think it's a massive opportunity for sport and a massive opportunity for St Johnstone to really capitalise on what they have done to help the next generation.

Alastair Blair
Club Historian

Dazed in May

In May 2020, with the previous season having been called and Saints shunted up one place into the top six, to the chagrin of Hibs' fans (something the latter would have to get used to in the next 12 months), I wasn't thinking too much about how we would get on in the new season.

This is because Brian Doyle and I were taking advantage of the lull in all kinds of social, economic and leisure activity to steamroller ahead with our new book, with the working title 'The 60 Greatest Saints' (*Hagiography* as a title came later). Over the spring and summer, I was interviewing and writing furiously – something I suspect the author of this book will empathise with – and throughout the autumn we were organising printing and publication. And at the same time, we were getting used to watching Saints on the TV screen and, increasingly, missing dreadfully the actual experience of being able to attend a match in person.

Add in the fact that the team was not exactly firing on all cylinders (I was also trying to maintain my business) and it should have been a stressful time, but in reality it was actually pretty good. I had the advantage over virtually all other Saints' fans of being able to speak with Callum, Macca and the various players who feature in *Hagiography*. The consensus, from the manager down, was that the team's performances were good and, although we were not winning, that would change.

Brian and I would speak at half-time and full-time in most of our games, and I also shared conversations and texts with Stewart McKinnon, who, as well as being my accountant and friend, is also one of the most vocal St Johnstone fans of the last 30 years. I also enjoyed the post-match Facebook rants of

Gordon Muir, who possibly even edges Stewart when it comes to stentorian, forthright, constructive criticism of the team and management. The general feeling amongst us was that, although we were playing well, we lacked a cutting edge and couldn't score in the proverbial.

Other than the obvious cup successes, the highlight of the season for me was being asked to do the co-comms at Kilmarnock on 30 January this year. I don't kid myself this was anything to do with my ability as a commentator, rather that I live seven miles from Rugby Park. With Saints losing 2-0 at half-time, the air was blue when Steven Watt switched off the mics at half-time, but three goals in the second half saw the mood change. I was told later that our commentary was a second ahead of the pictures, so watching fans knew we'd scored before they saw the ball actually hit the net.

Many will say that game at Kilmarnock was when we turned our season around, but with my club historian's hat on I'd actually trace it back to the previous season and another game at Kilmarnock – a hard-fought scoreless draw on a dark night, watched by fewer than 90 Saints' fans. Tommy Wright is gone now, but his work in transforming the team by dint of reducing the average age and bringing in some key players (Rooney and McCart in particular) as well as giving young Ali McCann a (fairly) regular game, was instrumental in creating the foundation that Callum and his team have built upon.

It was apparent that Callum's style of play was different though and, as the season progressed, it was obvious that there was a rising level of confidence in the system and how well we could both nullify opponents and (generally – so long as we scored first) go on to win the game.

In 2021, everything came together. Sneaking into the top six was brilliant but the cup final days were not so much the icing on the cake as a full-blown, medieval banquet lasting well into the next day if not beyond. Watching the games, the tension, in our house at least, was off the scale, but in retrospect, we actually won both relatively easily. Stuck in Ayrshire and unable to go out celebrating in Perth after the Scottish Cup win, we (my wife Helen and I) found a bottle of champagne and demolished it in about 20 minutes. We were still in a daze: could it really be that St Johnstone had completed a cup double? After winning the Scottish Cup in 2014, I thought that feeling could never be equalled, but now I know it can be surpassed. It is all down to Callum, his management team and a gloriously committed group of players, performing collectively at a level way above their individual talents, albeit we do have some very skilful players who will, I'm sure, go on to bigger clubs and more lucrative employment in the future. So to the management and the players, thank you: you have brought such joy to what, with the pandemic, has been a joyless period of our existence. Mind you, they completely stuffed up our rankings of the 'Greatest Saints' in *Hagiography* . . .

Jim Mackintosh
Makar of the Federation of Writers Scotland

The Belief

A Saturday in late May, near enough 5 o'clock
We all sat silent under the weight of history born:
Out of windows, over gardens, both ordinary and beer
Across roofs, empty streets, around blue corrugation
Where hallowed ground gently embraced our disbelief.

Our voices rose up tying joy to dream filled clouds
As if every sadness and every loss was forgotten

That late afternoon in May – the unlock of loyalty
Once called daftness because we were mocked
For our defence of the obvious – immortality beckoned.

An old man in a sharp grey suit
Smiling at me, thumbs up, turned towards the park.
A blue silk scarf with a white pinstripe folded
Neatly around his neck – my father's happy ghost
Wouldn't have missed this for all the pies in heaven.

When I first went to the Ormond games, he insisted
These were the golden years – never to be bettered.
He was right. We had shared them. The precious bond yet.
And the hallowed ground embraces all of us. I believe
Those were the golden years and here now they still are.

Ollie Wale
Singer-songwriter, 'Fair Maid'

I'm not a particularly superstitious person, but 32 has always
been my lucky number. I set the TV volume at 32 for the League
Cup Final before Shaun Rooney scored the winner in the 32nd
minute. I made sure that I did the exact same thing before the
Scottish Cup Final. Once again, Shaun Rooney scored the
winner in the 32nd minute. As soon as that goal went in, I had
full confidence we'd see it out.

I started attending Saints matches in 1997 or 1998. There
were some challenging moments ahead, but I've been fortunate
enough (by and large) to witness what has predominantly felt
like a club on a constant upwards trajectory. I assumed that
the Scottish Cup win in 2014 would be the denouement, the
pinnacle of this golden era, the final destination after everything

which Geoff and Steve Brown had been working towards for so long. Since then, we have been treated to multiple European qualifications and top-six finishes, culminating in the now legendary campaign of 2020-21. Surely this, now, is the pinnacle of our golden era? Does it get any better than this? It's fair to say that most people would have their doubts about that, but you can't rule anything out when it comes to this special club.

For multiple reasons, last season was extraordinary. We've had no choice but to watch St Johnstone on our television and computer screens every Saturday, unable to show our support (in person at least) for this talented young manager and his remarkable team. At the start of the season, when Saints were struggling to get results, this was a difficult thing to stomach. As the campaign wore on and it became clear that we wouldn't be able to properly celebrate it turning around to such an incredible extent, it became 10 times more challenging. A pandemic, Zander Clark's improbable heroics at both ends of the Ibrox pitch, Shaun Rooney's speedy ascent to 'cult hero' status, European qualification once again, and a trophy-laden finish. All of these things, and many more, have combined to make this particular triumph feel almost dreamlike. Such is the unbelievable and surreal nature of it, I'm still not sure whether it has fully sunk in.

I'll admit to occasionally feeling a tinge of sadness that we couldn't be there to see it in person. Whenever I feel this way, I like to remind myself that events almost certainly wouldn't have unfolded in the exact same manner if we had been there. A lone shout from the crowd could encourage a player to pass to someone on his left rather than his right, or to make a decision more quickly than he otherwise would have done, and suddenly a completely different set of circumstances begins to unfold. I am glad that this particular set of circumstances unfolded, providing us with memories which might never have existed otherwise. And how many people can say that their club won a cup double during a global pandemic? In a strange, bitter-sweet way, it only serves to make this era feel even more memorable and significant.

People say that football is just a game. At surface level, they'd be correct. But everything in life is 'just' something unless you're passionate about it. Football is one of my biggest passions and I honestly don't know where I'd be without it, especially after this past year. It's no exaggeration to say that football has probably helped many people to climb out of the negative mental spiral they'd fallen into.

We won the cup double. It's the greatest season in our history and, given our budget, arguably the greatest domestic season for any club in Scottish football history. In a sense, it's a shame that the fans weren't there to see it in the flesh. On the other hand, it couldn't have been more timely. Thanks to Callum Davidson and this squad of players for providing us with our best season of all-time during a year which has occasionally felt like the worst of all-time in other respects. Thank you, St Johnstone.

Roddy Grant
Director, Former Striker

It was very exciting at the start of the season going to all the games. I was obviously privileged and it was excellent to be there. But it was hard going, with no atmosphere and such a terrible thing that the fans couldn't get to the games.

It's therefore absolutely fantastic what the players achieved without the support of the fans. We played with a freedom, an enjoyment and a smile on our face. As soon as Callum took over, he set a system he wanted to play and credit to him. At the start of the season, we weren't getting the rub of the green, losing by the odd goal, but he persevered with it. All the players bought into the system he wanted to play, with a high press and such like. He deserves so many plaudits, as a lot of people might have panicked, but he stuck to his guns which I thought was absolutely fantastic.

I think the run of games in the second half of the season helped the players. Players like to play games, you are always up for it and sharp. Callum had a settled side. Fair enough, he had to bring players in for suspensions and injuries and such like, but the nucleus was there.

When he did have to change things, any player that came in knew exactly what to do in the same system. They did exactly the same job. The bigger clubs down south, or the Old Firm, tend to rotate their teams, such are their squad sizes, but a settled team definitely helped Callum.

You look at the game at Easter Road late in the season when we had to make a few changes, but we still played the same way and we managed to beat Hibs again. The confidence just grew and grew in the squad. It was the same at Ibrox in the cup quarter-final. That success must have given the team so much belief. It was thoroughly deserved as well. We matched them and then came back after losing such a late goal. It was a special night. It was just a fantastic season.

The way the club has handled Covid as well has been first class. It was regimental what we all had to do, players and staff. OK, we had a wee scare the week before the cup final, but I think it has been a credit to the club and everyone involved.

I've been at the club 11 years behind the scenes, doing various jobs. I think back to my playing days here too and it's a special place. However, I don't think I ever saw this happening. This is a feat, in my opinion, that will never ever be done again by a club outside the Old Firm, including Aberdeen. That just shows you the magnitude of the achievement. I've heard people say it's a bigger achievement than Leicester winning the English Premier League and I totally agree with that.

It's been great taking the trophies out into the community. It's been a little surreal. It's just amazing what Callum and the players have achieved.

Steven Watt
SaintsTV Commentator

Saints have been a massive part of my life for as long as I can remember. I've followed the club through some highs and many lows. You'll know well how good those highs feel and how rotten the lows are.

On 22 May 2021, I was amongst the very privileged ones able to witness us reaching our ultimate high. My journey started at Kelty Hearts, our first Betfred League Cup group stage match and finished with Jason Kerr lifting the Scottish Cup amidst scenes of joy and disbelief at Hampden. What an adventure!

The opportunity to commentate for SaintsTV allowed me a VIP seat as we strode towards our dream double. Playing a tiny part in this story is something I'm eternally grateful for. My commentating CV is hardly illustrious, a fan with the mic.

In the weirdness of the pandemic, going to the match was a bizarre experience. Pre-game questionnaires to complete, strict protocol to follow, temperature checks on arrival and of course, nae pals and fans to enjoy it with. Saints adjusted to empty stadiums tremendously well.

Me? Watching Saints was a treat, but football without fans is something I'd never get used to. There wasn't even the warming comfort of a half-time Bovril.

A highlight of the Betfred campaign came at a blustery Balmoor commentating on a match most were only able to watch on Peterhead's livestream, akin to watching football through a keyhole.

I had many 'pinch myself' moments during the campaign. From the obvious 'is this happening?' feelings of history being made to the surreal experience of commentating on Saints with guys sat by my side (two metres away) who I'd idolised from the stands.

The Betfred tie at Motherwell saw me joined by Peter MacDonald, a fella who I'd celebrated scoring a hat-trick at the same ground some years previously. His good luck continued that afternoon.

In the quarter-final at Dunfermline, I had the pleasure of long-standing Hospital Radio Perth match commentator John Watson on the mic, the narrow win setting up our semi-final tie v Hibs. An empty Hampden Park on a cold January Saturday can be a soulless place, that Saints chose to warm up that afternoon with a hammering of Hibs felt simply exquisite.

A controlled performance by the team against Livingston in the final, part one completed. The same control couldn't be said for the commentary team! On co-comms was Stuart Cosgrove, he hyped us all up with his excitement on the mic. A fellow lifelong Saintee, I knew just how much it meant.

A trip to Dens Park saw our Scottish Cup campaign up and running, without the normally magnificent Saints support making the trip. With fans' favourite Danny Griffin joining me, Saints grabbed the win, with Charlie Adam missing a spot kick for the hosts. Danny simply couldn't hide his pleasure at Zander's fine penalty save.

The Scottish Cup quarter at Ibrox saw my commentary silenced due to technical issues. Watching from the gantry at what unfolded left me speechless too. A massive highlight of my Saints supporting life.

The sight of the players picking themselves off the turf after a late opener had looked to dash our hopes, the sight of the luminous green giant Zander Clark rising to nod goalward and the delirium etched on the players' and management team's faces as Ali slotted home the vital penalty. The double dream was alive, maybe it was meant to be?

With a trip to Hampden now a strangely familiar experience, the semi against St Mirren felt like we would falter. The only other team to triumph over Rangers domestically and a side who had enjoyed an upturn in fortunes. Taking my position at the back of the North Stand, it felt like deja vu striking. That winning feeling once again, the fan reaction being the one HUGE miss.

Hibs were the final favourites, just the way we like it. It seemed written in the stars that we would triumph. Our habitual bridesmaid tag having been shaken off now. The feelings at full time were incredible, listening back I was lost for words, my co-commentator, fellow Saints Media volunteer Ross Gardiner, left to help piece together what had happened. The pinnacle of our history summitted.

Thanks to Saints for believing in me and giving me the opportunity on SaintsTV, and to those who provided co-commentary. Huge thanks too for the support and positiveness this Saints fan-turned-commentator received over the course of our extraordinary season.

Kieran Clark
St Andrews

It did not seem real. How could it have been? When the final whistle blew at the Scottish Cup Final, I had no idea how to react. There was no precedent for an achievement like this. Not for St Johnstone. Not for any club of this size.

During the wee small hours of Sunday morning, I rewatched the televised coverage, reliving the build-up, the key moments, and the post-match celebrations. As the sun rose the next day before my bleary and admittedly teary eyes, only THEN did it begin to sink in.

This was something beyond a dream – I had never before considered the possibility of a double. Winning a major trophy had been the lifelong hope – something that was unforgettably achieved in May 2014. Securing another – this time the League Cup in February – was magical for different reasons, an unexpected validation that it wasn't a one-off and could happen again. But what happened next – no one saw coming.

Leaving McDiarmid Park on 7 March 2020 after the final game before the shutdown, I couldn't have imagined that it would be over a year without watching Saints in person. Unthinkable. The pandemic separated us from the things that we hold dearest; family, friends, and yes, even (and especially) our football club.

Living miles from Perth and with the future uncertain, I wondered if there would be a growing sense of detachment as the months of separation passed – which is quite a confession from a passionate season ticket holder of two decades – but I can honestly say that I have never felt more connected to St Johnstone than I do now.

Football is escapism, I've long viewed it as the purest form of theatre. It's pantomime for adults – you've got everything in there. Thrills, excitement, drama, and there can be a fair degree of tragedy too, at times. There's also absurdity and humour. And we all needed that package more than ever.

Watching your team on TV, a laptop or an iPad may be a compromised experience, but it was essential and became more intimate. As our own lives were restricted, we invited Callum Davidson (in my mind the greatest all-round figure in St Johnstone folklore) and his players into our homes every week, seeing them grow in stature as the season progressed, the style of play eventually being rewarded, and the odd break gratefully falling in our favour, before embarking on an exhilarating journey that surpassed any television drama that you may have binged.

And my goodness, what a payoff this series had. I believe the winning goal against Hibernian encapsulated everything about our side – the sheer determination of Callum Booth's double tackle, the trademark skill and quality of local lad turned three-time cup winner David Wotherspoon, and Shaun Rooney once again channelling his supernatural ability to be in the right place on the big occasion.

Not a group of passing mercenaries, this is a team that is engrained within the club, dominated by those who were developed through it and by legends who have become part of the fabric. All of them now heroic figures. And it was genuinely moving to see Liam Craig and Murray Davidson – two of the greats – finally claim deserved glory.

We couldn't be there to see it happen, an unfortunate circumstance of this era, but we all witnessed history, a timeless gift, and we will forever – always – have our own stories to share.

Jim Eccleston
Carlops, Scottish Borders

Being a St Johnstone supporter has never been an easy option. Sure, we've had some really great spells in our history – the pre-WW2 Saints team, the late 60s/early 70s Willie Ormond team, the late 90s team of Sturrock and Clark – and then the team we've been blessed with over the last 10 years. But in between times, in common with all provincial clubs, there have been extremely barren spells – years of mediocrity – though this makes the successful spells extra special!

I think we all thought that the pinnacle of supporting Saints was Celtic Park on 17 May 2014 – nothing could or would ever surpass that for a Saints fan. But then in 2021, something quite extraordinary happened during the darkest days of a global pandemic that had seen us all confined to our homes with minimal human contact for so much of the time. The best way to describe the 2020-21 Scottish football season is that of a modern day football miracle. Amazing achievements happen in football – from Leicester City winning the English Premiership to the emergence of village team Castel di Sangro into the upper reaches of Italian football in the late 1990s. But these miracles always happen somewhere else – to somebody else's team. That was until 2020-21, when our very own St Johnstone were centre stage and realised the impossible dream of a cup double.

What did it mean to me? Well, on 22 May, immediately after the dust had settled, my thoughts were with the many Saints fans who had gone before us, who had hopefully watched this miracle unfold from the 'Ever After Stands' in the sky. My own dad passed away in 2016 – he was a season ticket holder for 50+ years and took me along to my first game in the mid-1970s and passed on that Saints bug to me. He eulogised about the wonders of Paddy Buckley and then the Ormond greats from the late 1960s. Before each of the finals, I had a quiet word with him to help settle the nerves – and then thought about him tearfully afterwards, wishing I could just give him a call or a hug in celebration.

And I thought of all these other great Saints fans who followed the team through the leanest of lean years but never lost the faith. Tears fell down my cheeks as I thought of the intense pride they would have felt. And also those greats who wore the shirt but are no longer with us – especially the ones I idolised from the terraces of Muirton in my youth – big Drew Rutherford and the wonderful Don McVicar who gave their every last bit to the cause. I also thought of the greats who worked behind the scenes at Muirton and McDiarmid – long-time secretary George Bell, our wonderful 'tea ladies' – Aggie Moffat and her predecessor of many decades' service Mary Gibson. For me, these two cup wins were a tribute to all of them – players, officials and fans no longer with us. Just such sadness that they couldn't witness these new fruits of their love and devotion to our club.

Thank you to the legends of 2021 – you have brought pride and happiness to the club, its supporters and to the wider community – never more important than at such a difficult time for society. This context must never be forgotten – but equally we should all feel good in celebrating such success and the happiness it delivered at a time when reasons to be cheerful were in very short supply.

I have always been intensely proud to support St Johnstone – even in the darkest days of the mid 1980s when we had such a close association with the lowest echelons of league football. They were my team back then just as they are today. Success and failure will never change that. But in my wildest dreams I never, ever dreamt of success like 22 May 2021. Thank you, Dad – I will never be more grateful for you passing that baton on to me.

Liam Barn
Perth

Much uncertainty surrounded what the 2020-21 season could look like during Covid. Little could we ever have imagined that the season about to unfold would be the greatest in our club's history.

Early-season league results were frustrating to watch (mostly on my laptop) with plenty of hard work and enterprise not being rewarded with points. The League Cup brought greater joy with Saints progressing to a Hampden meeting with Hibs (our first semi-final at the national stadium in longer than I could remember). It felt really weird not being able to go to the game and the first 30 minutes was mostly watched on TV through my fingers as Hibs, it's fair to say, battered us. The game turned so quickly, though, and three outstanding goals later we were in the final against Livi. In normal times, it would be at this point phone messages would start flying around – who was buying the tickets, booking the bus and what the meet time would be in the pub. For this final, I managed to secure a socially distanced place on the patio at my folks' house and watched the game through their patio doors with my dad (who was fortunate enough to be inside)! A totally controlled and professional 90 minutes later and the League Cup was heading back to Perth for the first time.

Scottish Cup wise, an away win to Dundee kicked things off nicely. As it was squeezed into a much shorter period of the season than normal, it felt like there was a round pretty much every week. I followed the quarters on the radio and almost switched off when Rangers scored so late in extra time – glad I didn't as the boys had other ideas! The pre-final Covid outbreak in the squad was a real concern and I genuinely felt it was maybe too much of an ask to win another final, but they were immense with that man Rooney scoring the vital goal once again.

Four trips to Hampden in one season and not being allowed to attend any of them was really tough to take, especially as my dad was away for the 2014 final and we never got to go to it together either. It felt amazing and surreal watching both trophies being lifted by Jason – ecstatic at the achievements, but also a gnawing feeling in the pit of my stomach at not being there to witness it all first-hand. When at the game, you have 100% your own story of what unfolds before you – the sights and sounds of every second of the day are very much your own. On TV, you see and hear exactly the same as all the other viewers, and once the programme is finished, you are left alone with your thoughts instead of celebrating and re-living the highlights with friends and family inside the stadium, on the bus home and in the pub on your return.

I thought the interviews with the players after both finals were excellent, talking about the belief and togetherness of the squad and articulating their experiences so well – an absolute credit to the club. The class of 20-21 was simply outstanding and thanks to everyone connected with the club for giving me and Saints fans everywhere such incredible memories in such incredibly difficult times.

John Dunbar
Perth

We won the double and we could not even be there, but does it take away from what it means to me? Absolutely no chance.

St Johnstone have just had the best season ever in their history and we crouched around TVs and used streams to watch our heroes. Watching games with some of the best people I know and celebrating when we won the cups, I still had the same disbelief and emotions flying all over the place and plenty of joyful tears.

Supporters of a small club know success is not winning trophies, it is cup runs and finishing in the top six with a hint of Europe thrown in. I have seen relegation and cup wins. We have had everything as supporters. Some amazing players have worn a Saints shirt and I have had the privilege of seeing them and meeting them, heroes in my eyes.

From going on the supporters' bus when I was younger to meeting up with all my mates and having an away day and getting a train all over the country – great days. My best mates are all Saints supporters and the best bunch of lads you could ask for, we all have Saints tattoos as well. One lad even drives down with his kids from up north for home games and then later drives back home again. Six hours' driving just to come see his mates and see the Saints. I absolutely love it.

We travel everywhere together, even over to Spain and now have supporters of Spanish team Hercules CF flying Saints flags at their home games. Bumping into Spanish lads, talking football and creating a bond over both teams has just been mind-blowing.

Going to games when I was younger is just like now, you count down to the Saturday and the closer it gets the more excited you get, even if it's a game against smaller teams like St Mirren or Hamilton. Planning your week around Saints and getting excited to go and see them play. My son, Riley, is now getting the same way (some may say he has been forced) but seeing him cheer and scream when we score makes me so happy.

St Johnstone, to me and a lot of others, is like family, you quickly defend them when they get slagged off, you rub it in when you beat your rivals or the so-called big teams. Walking into work on a Monday after the Saints have won is a great feeling, making sure everyone knows. I love St Johnstone FC and that will never change.

AUTOGRAPHS

AUTOGRAPHS

AUTOGRAPHS